MW00811088

IN THE HOUSE
OF
TOM
BOMBADIL

C.R. WILEY

canonpress
Moscow, Idaho

Published by Canon Press
P.O. Box 8729, Moscow, ID 83843
800–488–2034 | www.canonpress.com

C.R. Wiley, *In the House of Tom Bombadil*
Copyright © 2021 by C.R. Wiley

Academic references and quotations from Tolkien's oeuvre are all used
with gratitude to the Tolkien Estate.

Unless otherwise indicated, all Scripture quotations are from the
ESV® Bible (The Holy Bible, English Standard Verison®), copyright
©2001 by Crossway, a publishing ministry of Good News Publishers.
All rights reserved. All quotations from the King James (authorized)
Version are marked KJV. All versions used by permission.

Cover design by James Engerbretson.
Interior design by Laura Storm.
Printed in the United States of America.

All rights reserved. No part of this publication may be reproduced,
stored in a retrieval system, or transmitted in any form by any means,
electronic, mechanical, photocopy, recording, or otherwise, without
prior permission of the author, except as provided by USA copyright law.

Library of Congress Cataloging-in-Publication Data

Wiley, Chris, author. | Birzer, Bradley J., 1967- writer of
  foreword.
In the house of Tom Bombadil / C. R. Wiley ; foreword by Bradley J.
  Birzer.
Moscow, Idaho : Canon Press, [2021]
LCCN 2021043498 | ISBN 9781954887022 (paperback)
Subjects: LCSH: Tolkien, J. R. R. (John Ronald Reuel), 1892-1973.
Lord of the rings. | Christianity in literature.
Classification: LCC PR6039.O32 L63856 2021 | DDC 823/.912—dc23
LC record available at https://lccn.loc.gov/2021043498

22 23 24 25   5 4 3 2

CONTENTS

FOREWORD

BRADLEY J. BIRZER

I've been in love with Goldberry since 1979.

Well, "love" might be too strong a word. To be certain, I've had a crush on her since then. Granted, I was only eleven at the time I first met her, but something about her captivated my imagination and has ever since.

> Then another clear voice, as young and as ancient as Spring, like the song of a glad water flowing down into the night from a bright morning in the hill, came falling like silver to meet them....
>
> Her long yellow hair rippled down her shoulders; her gown was green, green as young reeds, shot with silver like beads of dew; and her belt was of gold, shaped like a chain of flag-lilies set with the pale-blue eyes of forget-me-nots. About her feet in wide vessels of green and brown earthenware, white water-lilies were floating, so that she seemed to be enthroned in the midst of a pool.[1]

What's not to love? She is, in almost every way, the perfect embodiment of a water spirit, a holy Nimue, a non-native White Buffalo Woman, or a more organic Virgin Mary.

---

1. *The Lord of the Rings: The Fellowship of the Ring,* 2nd edition (1954; New York: Houghton Mifflin, 1994), 119, 121.

VIII

Equally important, as the Hobbits understood, Goldberry embodied grace itself. "Their eyes followed her, for the slender grace of her movement filled them with quiet delight."[2]

I'm also fairly certain the painting of Goldberry by the Brothers Hildebrandt—which appeared in the 1977 Tolkien Calendar—didn't hurt my image of her, either. To this day, aside from Tolkien's own paintings, it's my favorite visual depiction from Tolkien's entire mythology. In some mysterious way, the two brothers captured her essence in that painting. She is at once the purity of youth and the ancient goddess of wisdom.

I also really liked (and continue to like) Tom Bombadil. I never minded his outlandish appearance. In fact, I thought his primary colors fit the majesty of his character. Plus, he helped my heroes, Frodo, Sam, Merry, and Pippin, just when their need was greatest. What was there not to like? My only disappointment on my first read of *The Lord of the Rings* was that I didn't get to see more of the man! That is, presuming he's a man. Certainly, I found him as interesting as I found Gandalf, and I loved Gandalf.

I can also state with certainty that after teaching *The Lord of the Rings* for two decades that no topic elicits more discussion from students than exactly who Bombadil is. Is he God? Is he a man? Is he a Vala or Maia that went native? Is he an unfallen Adam? Just who is he?

Whatever else he is, Bombadil is an excellent steward. In his own description of the land over which he is master, he says:

> There were fortresses on the heights. Kings of little kingdoms fought together, and the young Sun shone like fire on the red metal of their new and greedy swords.

---

2. *The Fellowship of the Ring*, 122.

There was victory and defeat; and towers fell, fortresses were burned, and flames went up into the sky. Gold was piled on the biers of dead kings and queens; and mounds covered them, and the stone doors were shut; and the grass grew over all. Sheep walked for a while biting the grass, but soon the hills were empty again. A shadow came out of dark places far away, and the bones were stirred in the mounds. Barrow-wights walked in the hollow places with a clink of rings on cold fingers, and gold chains in the wind. Stone rings grinned out of the ground like broken teeth in the moonlight.[3]

Despite all of this, Bombadil remains the master of his land, tempering its lingering evil. One might readily compare Bombadil's lands with those on the outskirts of Mordor.

Frodo looked round in horror. Dreadful as the Dead Marshes had been, and the arid moors of the Noman-lands, more loathsome far was the country that the crawling day now slowly unveiled to his shrinking eyes. Even to the Mere of Dead Faces some haggard phantom of green spring would come; but here neither spring nor summer would ever come again. Here nothing lived, not even the leprous growths that feed on rottenness. The gasping pools were choked with ash and crawling muds, sickly white and grey, as if the mountains had vomited the filth of their entrails upon the lands about. High mounds of crushed and powdered rock, great cones of earth fire-blasted and poison-stained, stood like an obscene graveyard in endless rows, slowly revealed in the reluctant light.[4]

Both places were the sites of formal and deadly battles—each meaningful in the history of Middle-earth—and, yet, the results were radically different. Bombadil was able to

3. *The Fellowship of the Ring*, 128.
4. *The Two Towers*, 2nd edition (1954; New York: Houghton Mifflin, 1994), 617.

reign over his land and have command of it through proper spells, taming it. No Bombadil existed for the outskirts of Mordor, however, and the land became so corrupt as to become nearly irredeemable, except through an act of God, perhaps by letting the ocean wipe it clean in a new flood.

Bombadil is so critical, he deserves his own book. . .

. . . And, Chris Wiley has done what is necessary. Indeed, he has done what is good, true, and beautiful.

With *In the House of Tom Bombadil*, Wiley brilliantly offers us some of the best insights ever made about J.R.R. Tolkien's invented world or, frankly, about 20th-century literature. Here is a book of intense wisdom and penetrating thought.

While I don't want to spoil the book—the reader should have the delight of reading Wiley directly—I would like to mention a few things about *In the House of Bombadil*.

First, it's a work of deep Christian humanism. That is, it asks the fundamental questions that every Christian who loves the humanities must ask: what is God; what is man; and what is man's relationship to God and man.

Second, while Wiley is always logical, he's never predictable. Just when you think he's going one way with a topic, he darts another way, but always as a joy for the reader.

Third, while Wiley offers wisdom, wisdom, and then more wisdom, he often does so—stylistically—in a humorous and casual manner.

Fourth, do not expect to have definitive answers as to who Bombadil or Goldberry are. When you complete this book, you will have more questions (all good ones) than certainties.

In other words, dear reader, you have in your hands a work of art, a gift to all of us. Have at it.

AN APOLOGY

THIS IS A short book; even so, I suspect that the subject's creator would think that it is too long and that the ideal page count should amount to zero.

I think that Professor Tolkien would have believed that I am up to no good. He didn't altogether approve of preachers, you know, being suspicious of us when we venture beyond our pulpits. He thought that we are particularly dangerous when we sit down to write stories, and he warned small children about us. Here's an example taken from his unpublished introduction to *The Golden Key* by the Reverend George MacDonald:

> I must warn you that [George MacDonald] is a preacher, not only on the platform or in the pulpit; in all his many books he preaches, and it is his preaching that is valued most by the grown-up people who admire him most.[1]

I think it is safe to conclude that Professor Tolkien didn't want children to grow up into the sort of people who read stories looking for preaching. Instead he wanted

---

1. *Smith of Wootton Major*, ed. Verlyn Flieger, 2nd ed. (1954; New York: Harper-Collins, 2005), 71–2.

children, as well as adults, to be taken up into stories, to experience the wonder, the mystery, and even the terror that can be found in them.

Perhaps it will surprise you to learn that (for the most part) I agree with him. In a review of Tolkien's story "Smith of Wootton Major" (my favorite when it comes to his short stories, by the way), Roger Lancelyn Green said something about stories that Tolkien later thanked him for: "To seek for the meaning is to cut open the ball in search of its bounce."[2] Rubber balls are meant to be gratefully received and enjoyed. (Even preachers know that.) When it comes to Tolkien's stories, it's their bounce that he wanted us to enjoy.

And yet, balls can be admired and even talked about without cutting them open. Tolkien did that sort of thing himself quite famously in a talk he once gave titled "On Fairy Stories." In that talk we learn (obliquely) that what irritated the Good Professor when it came to preaching with stories was *allegory*. After repeatedly being accused of committing the sin of allegory in his own stories, he said this in the foreword to the second edition of *The Lord of the Rings*:

> I cordially dislike allegory in all its manifestations, and always have done so since I grew old and wary enough to detect its presence. I much prefer history, true or feigned, with its varied applicability to the thought and experience of readers. I think that many confuse 'applicability' with 'allegory'; but the one resides in the freedom of the reader, and the other in the purposed domination of the author.[3]

My intent with this book is to exercise my freedom as a reader. And taking Professor Tolkien at his word, I intend

2. Humphrey Carpenter, ed., *The Letters of J.R.R. Tolkien* (1981; New York: Houghton Mifflin Harcourt, 2000), 388.
3. *The Lord of the Rings: The Fellowship of the Ring*, xv.

to apply Bombadil to all sorts of things, not the least being principled resistance to "purposed domination."

But I'm getting ahead of myself.

Back to the matter of application, while allegories can artlessly shove meanings beneath our noses, there is no such thing as a story without some kind of morality running through it. And when it comes to fairy stories, the morality very often doesn't hide at all. Tolkien says something along this line when discussing the prehistoric origins of many fairy tales.

> Even where a prohibition in a fairy-story is guessed to be derived from some taboo once practised long ago, it has probably been preserved in the later stages of the tale's history because of the great mythical significance of prohibition. A sense of that significance may indeed have lain behind some of the taboos themselves. Thou shalt not—or else thou shalt depart beggarded into endless regret. The gentlest 'nursery-tales' know it. Even Peter Rabbit was forbidden a garden, lost his blue coat, and took sick. The Locked Door stands as an eternal Temptation.[4]

Speaking of temptation, *The Lord of the Rings* is a story about temptation. It's impossible to miss. Of course, I'm speaking of the Ring of Power and the Temptation to Use It.

Tolkien was not the first to conceive of a ring that can make its wearer invisible. He wasn't even the first to note that such a thing would inevitably be used for wicked things. Another well-known story of this kind is told in book two of Plato's *Republic*. It is the story of "The Ring of Gyges."

The moral of that story is that a ring that would make a wearer invisible would inevitably reveal the wickedness of the wearer. The subject for discussion at this point in

---

4. "On Fairy Stories," *in Tree and Leaf* (London: Allen and Unwin, 1964), 33.

Republic is the nature of justice, and Socrates, the great protagonist of Plato's dialogues, is speaking with a fellow named Glaucon. Glaucon cynically contends that justice is nothing but an agreement among people who want to "get away with murder" but who are all afraid of being murdered. And Glaucon uses the story of the ring of Gyges to make his point.

According to Glaucon's telling of the tale, the ring of Gyges was found by a shepherd on the corpse of a giant. Then the lucky finder soon discovers the power of the ring to render him invisible, and being an ambitious fellow, he uses it to secure a position in the royal court. Before long he has seduced the queen, killed the king, and become king himself. The moral of the story is to keep an eye on shepherds, and everyone else, because you never know what they'll do if you don't—such is the sum of justice.

While the ring of Gyges is a powerful ring, the Ring of Power in *The Lord of the Rings* is even more impressive. Not only can it render you invisible—get this—it gives you the power to bend other people to your will.

It had been forged by Sauron—a giant, I suppose you could say—but not physically: it's his power that is gigantic. Like evil giants everywhere (including those real ones in our world), he is hell-bent on dominating everything around him. But unlike you or me, he actually has the power to get the job done. When he made his Ring, Sauron poured enough of himself into it so that anyone who put it on would have access to his power.

But here's the catch: all this bending includes the wearer of the Ring. That's the other important difference from the ring of Gyges. That ring merely revealed how bad people are; the Ring of Power actually makes its wearer worse. In time he comes to resemble its maker.

The Ring of Power isn't neutral, like sweet cream, to which someone's personality can be added to make a new flavor of ice cream. It is *malum in se*—intrinsically evil. It is inalterably bent in a particular direction. In other words, the Ring cannot be put into the service of a good cause. Throughout the story the notion that it could be used for good is the temptation that snares otherwise noble characters. And once snared, they are bent by the Ring until they conform to its intrinsic nature.

But there is one curious exception; we learn that the only person over whom the Ring cannot exercise a corrupting influence is the only person who would never, ever, think of using it for any reason whatsoever.

As you may already know, this book is about that person. And it is the bounce in his step that I admire and I'd like to talk about. I hope that I don't cut him open, or even bend him, in the process.

And if Professor Tolkien ever picks up this book, I hope that he will forgive this preacher for wondering aloud about the joyful bounce of Bombadil.

If you've forgotten that bounce, read the tale that Tolkien told about him again. It isn't long. Much of what I have to say about him is found in the first volume of *The Lord of the Rings*, *The Fellowship of the Ring*, in the chapters titled "The Old Forest," "In the House of Tom Bombadil," and "Fog on the Barrow-downs."

~ *C.R. Wiley*

CHAPTER I

"WHO IS TOM BOMBADIL?"

YOU EITHER LOVE him or hate him, or so it seems. For readers in a rush, Tom Bombadil feels like a needless insertion, a detour, or maybe a way to buy time for an author who is unsure of what comes next. How does he advance the plot, anyway?

If a threadbare story is what you're after, and a thrilling race to the finish, then there doesn't seem to be much of a point to Bombadil. He might as well be left out of *The Lord of the Rings*. That's what Peter Jackson did with his film adaptation.

But J.R.R. Tolkien didn't write a thriller, even though it is thrilling. It's *more* than that, and that's why people thrill to read it again and again. Most thrillers skim along the surface, each thrill topping the last. Speed is essential. But if you know what comes next, the thrill is gone. However, *The Lord of the Rings* is better the fourth or fifth time through, and that's saying a lot, because reading it just once can change your life. It changed mine.

The Lord of the Rings is a deep book. It's the depth that justifies re-reading, because the reader misses so much the first time through. (And the second, third, fourth, and fifth times through.)

But even people who have read *The Lord of the Rings* with patience and attention to detail can lose patience when it comes to Bombadil. What's the point of the enigmatic and apparently ridiculous fellow in the blue jacket and yellow boots? What purpose could he possibly serve? Even characters in the story are as mystified by him as the reader. And scholars who have plumbed the depths of Tolkien's legendarium[1] are flummoxed when asked, *"Who is Tom Bombadil?"*

So, who is Tom Bombadil?

Let's begin with his appearance. I mean both his physical appearance and his appearance in the story. Here's his entrance. This is from *The Fellowship of the Ring*, the first volume of the trilogy, from the chapter titled "The Old Forest."

> Then suddenly, hopping and dancing along the path, there appeared above the reeds an old battered hat with a tall crown and a long blue feather stuck in the band. With another hop and a bound there came into view a man, or so it seemed.

Tolkien then describes an odd creature—someone too big to be a hobbit, yet too small to be a man. That's a subtle hint, I think. Tom is *sui generis*—he's a breed apart. Furthermore, he's loud, not just in speech, but in manner. Hobbits are wary, and even stealthy, as any small creature with an interest in survival should be. But Tom is heedless,

---

1. The legendarium is the enormous backstory of *The Lord of the Rings*. It covers thousands of years and contains hundreds of characters. If that seems like it would take a lifetime to come up with, that's because it did.

and I think that this is another clue. He doesn't care who knows he's coming—in fact, he announces it. Then the Good Professor tells us more:

> He had a blue coat and a long brown beard; his eyes were blue and bright, and his face was as red as a ripe apple, but creased into a hundred wrinkles of laughter. In his hands he carried on a large leaf as on a tray a small pile of white water-lilies.[2]

Well, he does appear odd, but he seems nice enough. He turns out to be better than nice; he turns out to be good, and just as importantly, surprisingly powerful—he's just what a hobbit needs when he's at the mercy of a malevolent willow-tree.

Speaking of trees, the dilemma the hobbits face when Tom shows up is itself a bit surprising because Tolkien was something of a tree-hugger.[3] Frodo, Sam, Merry, and Pippin have gone into the Old Forest to escape the pursuit of black riders—black figures on black horses. The story has hardly begun, and the four hobbits that the story follows are nearly done in by a willow-tree. But the Forest proves to be nearly as dangerous as the riders. Later we're told that even though trees are large, and strong, they're not invulnerable. Things that move about on two legs, or four, or even more, prey on them: eating them, cutting them down, burning them. But they remember when they were the Lords of the forest. And this combination of age, memory, and malice has made them dangerous, especially

---

2. *Fellowship of the Ring*, 117. Douglas Wilson once pointed out to me that the most common color in *The Lord of the Rings* is grey—Grey Havens, grey eyes, Gandalf the Grey, etc. But he noted that when Bombadil appears, he comes in the primary colors: yellow, blue, and red. He's the full spectrum. This will be important when I contrast him with someone else in *The Lord of the Rings*.
3. For a marvelous treatment of Tolkien's ecological vision, see Matthew Dickerson and John Evan's book *Ents, Elves, and Eriador: The Environmental Vision of J.R.R. Tolkien* (Lexington, KY: University of Kentucky Press, 2011).

the Great Willow, the most powerful tree in the Old Forest. He holds the other trees under his sway—his songs are "invisible root-threads" that pull other trees along after him according to his will.

It is while the hobbits are under the spell of the willow that Tom Bombadil comes romping and stomping along. We learn his name before we even seen him because the fellow can't stop singing about himself. As he comes traipsing by, this is what the hobbits hear:

> *Hey dol! merry dol! ring a dong dillo!*
> *Ring a dong! hop along! fal lal the willow!*
> *Tom Bom, jolly Tom, Tom Bombadilo!...*[4]

This is just a snippet of what he sings—and it has the feel of something impromptu. It not only describes him, it announces his intentions. He is going home to his beloved Goldberry, and he's bringing something important—white water-lilies. And he's in a hurry—so watch out Willow-man!

When Tom arrives on the scene Merry's feet are sticking out of a crack in the tree, and Pippin has been swallowed alive. Frodo and Sam run up to Tom begging for help. Tom then, with what amounts to mock alarm, asks:

> 'Whoa! Whoa! Steady there!' cried the old man... 'Now, my little fellows, where be you a-going to, puffing like a bellows? What's the matter then? Do you know who I am? I'm Tom Bombadil!'[5]

After Frodo and Sam tell Tom about their predicament, Tom says this:

---

4. *Fellowship of the Ring*, 116, 117.
5. *Fellowship of the Ring*, 117.

'What?' shouted Tom Bombadil, leaping up in the air.
'Old Man Willow? Naught worse than that, eh? That
can soon be mended. I know the tune for him. Old grey
Willow-man! I'll freeze his marrow cold, if he don't
behave himself. I'll sing hit roots off. I'll sing a wind up
and blow leaf and branch away. Old Man Willow!'[6]

And that's pretty much what Tom does—with the
exception of a wind blowing leaves and branches away.
He puts his mouth to the crack containing Merry, and
he sings in a low voice. Evidently that produces an effect:
Merry's legs begin to kick. Then Tom says:

'You let them out again, Old Man Willow!... What be you
a-thinking of? You should not be waking. Eat earth! Dig
deep! Drink water! Go to sleep! Bombadil is talking!'[7]

Then Tom takes one of its fallen limbs and beats the
tree with it—but that's not what does the trick; there's no
mistake—it's the singing that sets the hobbits free. Soon
Tom is pulling Merry out of the tree by his feet, and Pippin
is (in effect) kicked out by the tree itself.

After that, the Great Willow shudders and is still. In all
of *The Lord of the Rings* there's no other deliverance so
amusing, yet so striking. (Well, there is one other, but it is
also Bombadil's doing—and that can wait.)

After this, the capering and boisterous Tom invites the
hobbits to his house, and then, without waiting for them,
he bounds away and out of sight.

The bewildered hobbits trudge along after, and just as
the sun is going down, making the way difficult to see,
they spy Tom's house in the distance. A door opens, light
streams out, and Tom's wife, Goldberry—a figure nearly

---

6. *Fellowship of the Ring*, 117.
7. *Fellowship of the Ring*, 118.

as mysterious as Tom—sings them the rest of the way home. Once they cross the threshold they hear, "Come dear folk!... Laugh and be merry! I am Goldberry, daughter of the River."[8]

With the grace of a ballerina, she then shuts the door and bars it with her arms. Then she comforts the hobbits, promising that wild things, and shadowy things, cannot come in. Then she says, "Fear nothing! For tonight you are under the roof of Tom Bombadil."[9]

What follows is a delightful stay lasting two nights and a day. The house of Tom Bombadil proves to be as safe as the land surrounding it is perilous. Speaking of peril, not only is the house hemmed in by the old and malicious trees of the Forest, it is nestled right in the valley of the shadow of death. Rising behind the house are the Barrow-downs, a series of hills, which are the home to a series of burial mounds for forgotten kings; and among those mounds is at least one creature that the hobbits will soon meet and wish that they hadn't.

So I've finally got you where I want you. We're in the house of Tom Bombadil. Now I can return to the question that serves as the title to this chapter: *Who is Tom Bombadil?*

As I've already said, the hobbits are just as puzzled by Tom's appearance as the reader is, but the first to raise the subject of Tom's identity is Tom himself. When he asks them, "Do you know who I am?" he's giving everyone permission to wonder.

Significantly, the second person to wonder aloud about Tom is Frodo—the Ring-bearer, and primary protagonist of the story. And the person to whom he addresses his question is the person who knows Tom best, his wife, Goldberry.

---

8. *Fellowship of the Ring*, 121.
9. *Fellowship of the Ring*, 121.

Here's her response: "He is."[10]

Anyone familiar with the Bible, and especially the book of Exodus, can't help hearing in Goldberry's answer an echo of the words that came from the burning bush. When Moses asked a similar question the voice from the bush replied, "I AM THAT I AM."[11]

This has led some of Tolkien's more intrepid fans to suggest that the Bombadil is none other than Illúvatar incarnate, the One, the creator of Middle Earth in Tolkien's legendarium.

There are reasons for thinking that they may be right, and one very big one for knowing that they are not.

One thing in favor of the Illúvatar hypothesis is the fact that Tolkien was a very serious Roman Catholic. And even though religion in the forms we generally associate with it—you know, temples, and rituals and the like—are almost completely absent in *The Lord of the Rings*, Tolkien described the story as a fundamentally Catholic work.[12]

If Bombadil is Illúvatar, then a number of odd things about him might be explained. But other things wouldn't be. Even so, the best reason for dismissing the Illúvatar hypothesis is that Tolkien did. Here's what he said on the subject as it pertains to *The Lord of the Rings*: "There is no embodiment of the One, of God, who indeed remains remote, outside the World."[13] If we take him at his word— and I'm all for that—that settles the matter. Bombadil isn't the Creator; he's a creature, like the rest of the characters in *The Lord of the Rings*—and like you and me in our world.

This is a good spot to review a few of the other theories that people have come up with to explain Bombadil. One

---

10. *Fellowship of the Ring*, 122.
11. Exodus 3:14 (KJV).
12. What Tolkien meant by this is itself the subject of many essays and even some books. For example, see Bradley Birzer's book *J.R.R. Tolkien's Sanctifying Myth: Understanding Middle-earth* (Wilmington, DE: ISI Books, 2002).
13. Carpenter, 235.

of them—which is no explanation at all—is that Tom was inspired by a Dutch doll in the Tolkien home that had the misfortune of almost being flushed down the lavatory.[14] The reason this explains nothing is the same reason scientific explanations of natural phenomena that reduce everything to material causes explain nothing. They substitute a means for an end. The end in this case is the purpose Bombadil serves in the story. Saying that Tom Bombadil was inspired by a Dutch doll tells us nothing about that.

But what these two very different explanations actually do (namely, Bombadil is really Illúvatar, or Bombadil is just a Dutch doll) is they appeal to things outside of Middle Earth to explain the enigmatic man with the blue jacket and yellow boots. And I think that there is something to that.

Getting back to the Dutch doll hypothesis, the story goes that Tolkien made up Tom Bombadil initially to entertain and perhaps console his children. He even wrote a poem about Tom that predates the writing of *The Lord of the Rings* by years.[15] Then seemingly one thing led to another, and before you know it, he had inserted Tom into *The Lord of the Rings* either to suit his fancy or to buy time. That second notion seems to have some basis in fact because of Tolkien's admission that he was stumped for a while about the direction of the story just about the time he was writing about the hobbits in the Old Forest. Concerning that, this is what he said:

> I met a lot of things along the way that astonished me. *Tom Bombadil I knew already*; but I had never been to

---

14. Daniel Lauzon, "The Adventures of Tom Bombadil and Other Poetry," J.R.R. Tolkien Estate, https://www.tolkienestate.com/en/writing/other-tales-and-poetry/the -adventures-of-tom-bombadil-and-other-poetry.html.

15. The poem can be found in a collection of poems usually published under the title: *The Adventures of Tom Bombadil.*

Bree. Strider sitting in the corner of the inn was a shock, and I had no more idea who he was than Frodo did. The Mines of Moria had been a mere name; and of Lothlórien no word had reached my mortal ears till I came there. Far away I knew there were the Horse-lords on the confines of an ancient Kingdom of Men, but Fangorn Forest was an unforeseen adventure. I had never heard of the House of Eorl nor of the Stewards of Gondor. Most disquieting of all, Saruman had never been revealed to me, and I was as mystified as Frodo at Gandalf's failure to appear on September 22.[16]

But if Tom was just filler, why didn't Tolkien just go back and edit Tom out when he knew where things were headed? He was a notoriously fussy and precise writer. We know that he cut out huge swaths of material many times when he wasn't satisfied with them. But he left Tom in for a reason. And he said so in a letter.

> Tom Bombadil is not an important person—to the narrative. I suppose he has some importance as a 'comment'. I mean, I do not really write like that: he is just an invention (who first appeared in the *Oxford Magazine* about 1933), and he represents something that I feel important, though I would not be prepared to analyze the feeling precisely. I would not, however, have left him in, if he did not have some kind of function.[17]

So Tom does have "some kind of function"—and he is a "comment." What does Tolkien mean?

Generally speaking, people can sense that there is a lot more to *The Lord of the Rings* than what is visible on the surface. Throughout there are allusions to events and people found in a past that is ancient and remote even to

---

16. Letter to W. H. Auden, June 7, 1955, in Carpenter, 216–17, emphasis added.
17. Carpenter, 178.

characters in the story. There are layers upon layers of the stuff, much of it already written or sketched out by Tolkien by the time he came to write *The Lord of the Rings*.

And as I've already said, some of Tolkien's most devoted fans have combed through those stories looking to find the backstory of Bombadil. No such luck; he's just not there. But rather than give up, some of them have resorted to speculation. Working within the framework of the legend-arium, there has been the suggestion that Bombadil and his wife Goldberry are Maiar gone native.[18] (Maiar are elemental spirits, somewhat like angels, junior to other more powerful beings known as Valar,[19] but of the same nature.) When authorities on Tolkien weigh in on the matter, this seems to be a favorite explanation. And it appears to fit. We have other Maiar in *The Lord of the Rings*; a prime example is Sauron himself, the *Lord* in the title of the book. And we learn that Gandalf the wizard is one, as is Saruman, another wizard.

But if Tom has gone native, he's also gone a little rogue. I don't mean that in a bad sense. Obviously, he's good. I merely mean that he has his own agenda. He's not caught up in the story of the Ring. But even that doesn't feel quite right, and I'll explain why in chapter two. This brings me back to the idea that Tom may somehow be from Outside— meaning he represents something outside Middle Earth, or perhaps bigger than that world.

Two more theories I've run across that posit a version of the "Outside" argument are either that Tolkien has written himself into the story and he's Bombadil, or that Tom is the personification of the English countryside

---

18. Robert Foster, *The Complete Guide to Middle-earth: From the Hobbit to the Simlarillion* (London: HarperCollins, 1998).
19. Valar are like angels, creatures like us, but far more powerful than we are.

before industrialization. Concerning the second, Tolkien said as much in a letter to his publisher, Stanley Unwin.[20]

But will either of these possibilities really do?

The notion that Tolkien would make a cameo appearance doesn't seem plausible. A story that we can say reflects Tolkien's self-concept is *Leaf by Niggle*, where Tolkien is like Niggle, or better, where Niggle is like Tolkien—a little man prone to getting lost in the details—like obsessing over the way light is caught on an individual leaf—and undertaking projects far too large for him.[21] If that's so, how can we harmonize Bombadil's preternatural potency with Niggle's impotence? It doesn't seem possible. As for expressing the spirit of the English countryside, you might as well say that the Shire itself (the home of the hobbits) does this just as well, if not better.[22]

Instead, I believe that Tolkien was up to something else with Tom, something large and ambitious in its own way, something integral to the story as a whole. I even think that Tom is so important it would take a book to explain why. This book is my attempt to do this very thing.[23]

But before I begin, there's one proviso to make.

---

20. Carpenter, 1.

21. If you've never read *Leaf by Niggle*, I commend it to you. It is a beautiful fable, and a very Catholic one. Tolkien published it not long after *The Hobbit*, but years before *The Lord of the Rings*. In the story, Niggle has undertaken the project of painting a very large and beautiful tree. But he is afraid that he will never finish it, fearing it is both too ambitious for his skill, and that he will never have the time needed to work on it as he'd like. In the fable the painting isn't finished before Niggle has to go on a long journey. Then his painting is destroyed with the exception of one small leaf.

22. This summary of the theories proffered concerning Bombadil's origin and identity isn't meant to be exhaustive—it is merely intended to give you the gist of what people have said.

23. I can't say conclusively that what I have to say about Tom has never been said before, but as far as I know, I'm the first.

Enigma and Mystery

Would you be surprised to learn that Tolkien was sometimes enigmatic on purpose? He actually admitted that he was when it came to Bombadil. Here's the telling line from one of his letters: "even in a mythical Age there must be some enigmas, as there always are. Tom Bombadil is one (intentionally)."[24]

So, if Tolkien meant for Bombadil to be an enigma, who am I to try and clear things up? Well, I'm not sure that I can—at least not in the way most people think about clearing things up. But that doesn't mean that the Good Professor didn't intend for readers to ponder the meaning of Tom. Au contraire, enigmas invite inquiry. The word *enigma* comes into English in the 16th century via Latin, but originally from Greek. It means to "speak allusively," from αινος, for "fable." I'm sure Tolkien knew this, and I'm sure that he knew what happens when people stumble upon enigmatic things—they stop and wonder about them, particularly noble-minded people. As Solomon said, "It is the glory of God to conceal things, but the glory of kings is to search things out" (Prov. 25:2).

But you may think that this makes any guess a wild guess. But that presupposes we have nothing at all to work with. Tolkien said that Bombadil represented something important for him, something that he *wanted* us to see.

Here's something else to consider: Tom is more than enigmatic; he's also mysterious. Speaking of mystery, when someone mentions the word, we tend to get out our magnifying glasses, light our pipes, don our deer-hunter caps, and get set to practice the science of deduction. But this is a very modern way of thinking about mysteries. Tolkien wasn't Sir Arthur Conan Doyle.[25]

---

24. Carpenter, 174.
25. Although Doyle wrote several Sherlock Holmes stories before Tolkien was born, Holmes was the epitome of modernity in certain ways.

If you look into the etymology for the word *mystery*, you'll see that for time out of mind it referred to something other than a puzzle that needed solving. Like the word *enigma*, *mystery* comes into English from the outside— through the Old French *mistere*, but further back, from the Latin *mysterium*, and ultimately to the Greek *mysterion*. And at each step in the journey of the word down to our time, a mystery is not a problem; it is a hidden truth. Tom Bombadil is mysterious in this sense.

This is important to note before going any further because if you hope that this book will provide the final and definitive answer to the mystery of Tom Bombadil, you will be disappointed. When you've read the final line you won't be able to say, "Well, that solves that!" (At least I hope not.) The best mysteries are never solved. Solutions in the sense we associate with Sherlock Holmes are like equations that can be mastered, not things worth knowing for their own sakes. My hope is that you will come to love Tom for his own sake, and that the mystery of Tom Bombadil will haunt you for the rest of your life.

CHAPTER 2

"TOM BOMBADIL IS MASTER"

The future of our world depends on the contents of this chapter.[1]

I'm about to get into a hot topic—so hot I need to ease into it slowly and carefully, like a hot bath. What am I talking about? Let's return to the story.

The hobbits are now enjoying the atmosphere of a comfortable and well-ordered house. Goldberry attends to her domestic chores, but her movements are so graceful the hobbits sit entranced. And from the outside, Tom comically sings to himself. Then Frodo, no longer able to contain himself, asks the question you have already heard him ask, but here it is again, along with Goldberry's response, this time in context:

> 'Fair lady!' said Frodo again after a while. 'Tell me, if my asking does not seem foolish, who is Tom Bombadil?'
>
> 'He is,' said Goldberry, staying her swift movements and smiling.

---

1. By the time I'm done I hope you will see that this isn't hyperbole.

Frodo's incomprehension is plain to see, so Goldberry repeats herself, but she adds that Tom is master of "wood, water, and hill."

So Frodo naturally asks, "Then all this strange land belongs to him?"

Now it is Goldberry's turn to be puzzled. Frodo's inference that mastery means ownership doesn't follow for her. So she says:

> 'The trees and the grasses and all things growing or living in the land belong each to themselves. Tom Bombadil is the Master. No one has ever caught old Tom.... He has no fear. Tom Bombadil is master.'
>
> A door opened and in came Tom Bombadil. He had now no hat and his thick brown hair was crowned with autumn leaves. He laughed, and going to Goldberry, took her hand.[2]

There it is: Tom is *Master*. But his mastery is not the sort that Frodo is accustomed to. And Tom doesn't look like a master; he looks and sounds more like a jester. There's the blue jacket, the ridiculous yellow boots, the nonsense rhymes. There's a paradox to Tom's mastery. And everything in the world of Middle Earth (and I think our world as well) hinges on that paradox.

For the moment, let's focus on Goldberry's statement: "*Tom Bombadil is master.*" What could she mean if it doesn't imply ownership?

Remember, the Good Professor said that Tom represents something that he felt "important." Here he is again, in his own words:

> Tom Bombadil is not an important person—to the narrative. I suppose he has some importance as a "comment."

---

2. *Fellowship of the Ring*, 122.

I mean, I do not really write like that: he is just an invention (who first appeared in the *Oxford Magazine* about 1933), and he represents something that I feel important, though I would not be prepared to analyze the feeling precisely. I would not, however, have left him in, if he did not have some kind of function.[3]

Tolkien seems to dance around a bit here himself. At one moment he says that Tom Bombadil is a comment; then he says that he doesn't write like that. He also says that Bombadil isn't important; then he says that he represents something important. Why does he equivocate?

He's equivocating because he's trying to be clear without saying too much. Remember what he said about allegories? He "cordially" disliked them; he disliked them because they tend to be bossy, leaving little room for the reader to think for himself. That's because they work by simple one-to-one correspondences—THIS means THAT—as we see in *The Pilgrim's Progress*.[4] A lot of people think that if a story doesn't work this way it isn't saying anything important—it's just entertainment. But allegory isn't the only way to write meaningful fiction.[5]

Tolkien was a philologist—a connoisseur of languages. He knew all about speaking on more than one level without resorting to allegory. One way it can be done is by analogy. When something is an analog, it is both itself and like something else at the same time. In allegories characters don't really have lives of their own; they just represent other things; they're like cardboard standees. Analogs, on the other hand, are real in themselves. Characters in a story

---

3. Carpenter, 178.
4. As far as allegories go, John Bunyan's *The Pilgrim's Progress* may be the best ever written. Unfortunately, ever since it was published Christians have tried to imitate it without much success.
5. Not even entertainment is meaningless if we live in a meaningful world—and Tolkien certainly believed that our world is meaningful.

should have lives of their own, even if they remind readers of other things.[6] That's the essential difference between an allegory and an analogy: in an allegory the reader is at the mercy of the author; when it comes to analogy, the association is made in the mind of the reader—or not.

The characters in *The Lord of the Rings* are as rich as any you'll find in literature. But they can remind us of other people, sometimes from other stories. Or they can just remind us of things, such as courage or loyalty. So, what does Tom bring to mind? Well, with Goldberry's words in mind, allow me to make a suggestion: Tom can remind us of what dominion should look like.

Dominion without Domination

Dominion has gotten a lot of bad press. It's an odd thing in a way because without it we wouldn't have many of the things that make life livable.

The exercise of dominion in some sense is inevitable. After all, we must make a home for ourselves in the world—a *domus*, which is Latin for "home." *Domus*, by the way, is the source of the words *dominion, domination, domain,* and, of course, *domestic.* For Christians and Jews, and anyone else who believes in the God of the Bible, human beings have been given this world in order to make a home. Here's the pregnant passage from the Book of Genesis:

> So God created man in his own image,
> in the image of God he created him,
> male and female he created them.

---

6. By the way, you are an analog—and so am I. We are images of God, a subject I'll get to in a minute.

And God blessed them. And God said to them, "Be fruitful and multiply and fill the earth and subdue it, and have dominion over the fish of the sea and over the birds of the heavens and over every living thing that moves on the earth." (Gen. 1:27–28)

The Hebrew word that's translated "dominion" means something like "skilled mastery." And that's definitely what we see when we look at Tom. But skilled mastery can be a problem, as we see with the Ring of Power. When we see the Ring in action we see something very different than Tom Bombadil. When it comes to the Ring we see skill is used in a domineering way.

Going forward I'd like to reflect on the way that Tom exercises dominion, but I need someone to contrast him with. He needs a foil; or better, we can consider *Tom* to be a foil to our normal, which is to say, abnormal, way of thinking about dominion. (Think of it like a mirror, a foil flips things, providing an image in reverse, just like a mirror does.) So, who can we contrast Tom with in *The Lord of the Rings*? How about Sauron, the Dark Lord himself? Throughout *The Lord of the Rings* he looms in the background like a dark, malignant shade. But the problem with Sauron is this, when we look at him we just see a lidless eye looking back.[7] He's too remote to be useful in this regard; we don't really know enough about him.

Rather than Sauron, my candidate for Tom Bombadil's foil is Saruman. When it comes to him, we have material to work with. (And tellingly—his name means "man of skill.")

The corruption of Saruman is an important subplot running throughout *The Lord of the Rings*. We first learn of his fall from grace at the Council of Elrond. He had been a member of another council—the White Council—

7. Did Tolkien have in mind Jeremy Bentham, the father of utilitarianism—and the diabolical panopticon—when he envisioned Sauron as a "lidless eye"? I wonder.

and he had even been its chief.[8] But according to Elrond, Saruman's undoing had something to do with his long study of Sauron and his dark arts.

The degree to which he has been bent by those arts is revealed when he takes Gandalf captive; and it is in Gandalf's account of his captivity (and his escape) that we learn something important about Saruman's method of acquiring knowledge, and through knowledge, power.

Gandalf recalled how Saruman captured him by means of a skillful ruse. If that were not enough to reveal his fall from grace, at the Council of Elrond Gandalf recounts their conversation when the trap was sprung:

> "'You have come.... And here you will stay, Gandalf the Grey, and rest from your journeys. For I am Saruman, the Wise, Saruman Ring-maker, Saruman of Many Colours!"
>
> 'I looked then and saw that his robes, which had seemed white, were not so, but were woven of all colours, and if he moved they shimmered and changed hue so that the eye was bewildered.
>
> "'I liked white better," I said.
>
> "'White!" he sneered. "It serves as a beginning. White cloth may be dyed. The white page can be overwritten; and the white light can be broken."'[9]
>
> "'In which case it is no longer white," said I. "And he that breaks a thing to find out what it is has left the path of wisdom."'[10]

This is followed by Saruman's curt dismissal of Gandalf's insight into the nature of wisdom. Then he makes his own vision of what constitutes true wisdom starkly clear—it is the ability to see the "good" others

---

8. We learn later that the Lady Galadriel had misgivings about Saruman from the start and had actually wanted Gandalf to serve in this capacity.
9. Isaac Newton famously broke light into a spectrum with a prism in 1672. I suspect that this is a subtle reference to Newton's experiments with optics.
10. *The Fellowship of the Ring*, 252.

cannot see, and to accumulate power in order to force "fools" to comply with it.

Oddly, this is followed by Saruman's invitation to Gandalf to join him in his quest for power. But when Gandalf refuses Saruman coldly mocks him, informing him that he is now an unwilling "guest" who must remain with him until "the end." Gandalf asks: "Until what end?" "Until you reveal to me where the One may be found. I may find means to persuade you."[11]

We can guess what *that* means. Did you notice the telling line "the white light can be broken"? Saruman is willing to break more than light to learn what he wants to know.

Gandalf's statement about "break[ing] a thing to find out what it is" is a subtle yet profound allusion to a long debate on the nature of knowledge in the Western tradition.[12] Let's look at that.

Knowledge and Power

You've probably heard the statement attributed to Francis Bacon, "Knowledge is power." That's true so far as it goes, and power *can* be a good thing. But devils can hide in the nooks and crannies of otherwise good things.

One of the devilish things about knowledge today is that it has sued for divorce from wisdom. (They're not even on speaking terms in many minds.) Human wisdom was once believed to be based on a deeper wisdom written into the world, and it could only be acquired through dedicated and grateful converse with it. But for many modern people, there is nothing to be grateful for because there is no one

---

11. *The Fellowship of the Ring*, 253.
12. Gandalf in effect is saying that there are moral limits to what we can know, and that transgressing those limits is foolish—in other words, there will be Hell to pay.

to thank. Instead of wisdom, many people are after the facts that can be wrested from a stuttering and dim-witted world. This underlies much of what goes by the name "science" today. Perhaps surprisingly, Tolkien's good friend C. S. Lewis actually saw a connection between this and what used to be called magic.

> There is something which unites magic and applied science [technology] while separating both from the "wisdom" of earlier ages. For the wise men of old the cardinal problem had been how to conform the soul to reality, and the solution had been knowledge, self-discipline, and virtue. For magic and applied science alike the problem is how to subdue reality to the wishes of men; the solution is a technique.[13]

When the story of Western history is told, most historians leave out the strange fascination with magic that characterized the Renaissance.[14] That is supposed to have belonged to benighted times—like the "Middle Ages."

What does this have to do with Tom Bombadil? I think quite a bit.

The Lord of the Rings contains many things, and one of those things is an important distinction. Throughout *The Lord of the Rings* the Good Professor is careful to distinguish Dominion from Domination. We need to learn how to distinguish them for ourselves, because very often they get blended in unprincipled and tendentious ways. So, here's my point in a nutshell: *Tom is an image of what true dominion looks like.*

---

13. *The Abolition of Man* (New York: Macmillan, 1947), 48.
14. See Tom Shippey, "New Learning and New Ignorance: Magia, Goeteia, and the Inklings," in *Myth and Magic: Art According to the Inklings*, eds. Eduardo Sequra and Thomas Honegger (Zollikofen, Switzerland: Walking Tree Press, 2007), 22–46.

Is this really something that Tolkien had in mind when he wrote about Tom? Yes, I think so—at least in part. He could be very clear about his beliefs, especially in the context of anything he wrote on the subject of fairy tales. Take this for instance:

> The love of Faery is the love of love: a relationship towards all things, animate and inanimate, which includes love and respect, and removes or modifies the spirit of possession and domination. Without it even plain 'Utility' will in fact become less useful; or will turn to ruthlessness and lead only to mere power, ultimately destructive.[15]

In the modern world the quest for knowledge is premised on the belief that the natural world is nothing more than a vast machine. Since it is merely a machine, learning how it works entails disassembly, breaking things down into their constituent parts. Unfortunately for the things themselves, this is something of a downgrade from the ways they were once understood, everything from trees, to rivers, to people. Nothing is exempt. Now, because they are just things, they can be reassembled in novel ways. (Think Frankenstein's monster here.) All this is implicit in Saruman's attitude and behavior. He's a magician in the sense C. S. Lewis so aptly described in the earlier quotation from *The Abolition of Man*.

In contrast, Gandalf spoke up for an older way of knowing—a way that knows things without breaking them. In the old way of knowing, things are "more than the sum of their parts." (If you've heard that before, now you know what it refers to.) Hopefully you can see the wisdom in this way of knowing. After all, *you* are more than the sum of your parts. You are not a machine; you

---

15. *Smith of Wootton Major,* 131.

are a human being, with a name, and an identity, and a will of your own.

If you see the world the way Saruman does, you'll come to resemble a machine yourself. That's the way things work. Whatever we think is the final truth of things, that's the image we conform to. Later in *The Lord of the Rings* we're told that Saruman "has a mind of metal and wheels; and he does not care for growing things, except as far as they serve him for the moment."[16] But Saruman didn't start out that way. How he came to be that way should serve as a warning. (Hint: it was by studying the dark arts of the Enemy.)

Let's contrast this with Tom. Saruman's mind set a trap for Gandalf, but Tom set the hobbits free from Old Man Willow. What this demonstrates isn't just that Tom is good and Saruman isn't, but how two different understandings of knowledge work themselves out in different ways of life—one catches things to control them, and another frees them in order to commune with them.

When Frodo asked Goldberry "Then all this strange land belongs to him?" he had something like Saruman's attitude in mind; but when she said, "The trees and the grasses and all things growing or living in the land belong each to themselves. Tom Bombadil is the Master," she had Tom's wisdom in mind.[17]

"No one has ever caught old Tom"

Things belong to themselves, and yet there is a Master. Does that still strike you as odd? Think of it this way: Tom's mastery is limited. He doesn't own things, and he doesn't break them. Instead, he knows them in a very different way. In the next chapter I'll look into what Tom

16. *The Two Towers*, 462.
17. *The Fellowship of the Ring*, 122.

knows, but for the remainder of this one, let's look at what Goldberry said next: "No one has ever caught old Tom walking in the forest, wading in the water, leaping on the hill-tops under light and shadow. He has no fear."[18]

What can we say about Tom's freedom? Well, we can say at least one thing: it isn't freedom from responsibility. Tom cares about Goldberry; he cares about the hobbits; he even cares about their ponies. But the point here I think is this: Tom is nobody's fool and nobody's tool.

Let's go back to Saruman for a moment—he catches people so that he can use them. And he lied in order to catch Gandalf.

Saruman gloated when he noted that Gandalf had come at his summons. Gandalf mentions that it had been Radagast—another wizard—one less powerful than either Saruman or himself—who had conveyed the summons. This amuses Saruman.

> "'Radagast the Brown!' laughed Saruman, and he no longer concealed his scorn. "Radagast the Bird-tamer! Radagast the Simple! Radagast the Fool! Yet he had just the wit to play the part I set for him. For you have come, and that was all the purpose of my message. And here you will stay."'[19]

Radagast had been Saruman's tool, and that was because he was gullible—he was Saruman's fool.

Based on what we know about Tom, can we even imagine him doing such a thing? Tom doesn't set traps. He sets people free from them. Presumably Tom lives by the Golden Rule—no one can trap him, that's why he frees others. He has no fear, and he even frees other people from their fears—if sheltering the hobbits tells us anything.

---

18. *The Fellowship of the Ring*, 122.
19. *The Fellowship of the Ring*, 252.

Paradoxically, it's because Tom knows where he ends and other people begin that he's free. He knows his limits.

Limits are terribly frustrating for ambitious people. But limitless living isn't possible; thinking it is, is a kind of trap. We learn as the story goes on that Saruman has fallen into a trap himself, he is serving the Dark Lord. He has become Sauron's fool and tool. And we also learn that Saruman is full of fear—for good reasons.

Among the things that we see with Tom (at least so far!), the most surprising thing is what we don't see. The Ring of Power has no power over him. Here's the marvelous scene that reveals this:

> 'Show me the precious Ring!' [Tom] said suddenly in the midst of the story: and Frodo, to his own astonishment, drew out the chain from his pocket, and unfastening the Ring handed it at once to Tom.[20]

Tom then treats the Ring with a nonchalance, and even bemusement, that is without parallel in *The Lord of the Rings*. It seems to grow in his hand. He then peers through it like a monocle. He puts it on the little finger of one of "his big brown hands" and then admires it, like someone shopping for jewelry in a store. Then the hobbits realize, Tom hasn't disappeared! Instead, this follows: "Tom laughed again, and then he spun the Ring in the air— and it vanished with a flash. Frodo gave a cry—and Tom leaned forward and handed it back to him with a smile."[21]

There is so much I could say about this, but here are just a few observations. First, Tom *commands* to see the Ring. He doesn't ask; he doesn't say please; he says, "Show me the precious Ring!" And Frodo promptly does so. When others ask to see the Ring, in Rivendell with the Council,

---

20. *The Fellowship of the Ring*, 130.
21. *The Fellowship of the Ring*, 130.

for instance, or Boromir at Amon Hen, Frodo is reluctant; he resists. And Tom calls it "precious," calling to mind someone else's own word for it, but Tom does so almost mockingly.[22] Then, when Tom receives it, it seems to grow in his hand. This isn't the only time we see this happen: other times when it seems to grow it seems to indicate that the Ring is working to bring people under its spell. Then Tom isn't impressed. Then he holds it up to his eye, bringing to mind the eye of Sauron. Then Tom laughs. And then, so as to demonstrate that its power doesn't possess him, he places it on his little finger (note: his *little* finger), and nothing happens! He's as visible as ever, no disappearing for Tom. And later, when in a fit of spite Frodo puts it on *his* finger and attempts to sneak away from the table, the hobbits can't see him—but Tom can!

But most intriguingly, Tom performs a little magic himself. He makes the Ring disappear—like an uncle performing a trick for his nephews after dinner. Then, with a final demonstration of indifference, he casually hands the Ring back to Frodo.

No one can catch Ol' Tom—not even the Lord of the Rings. But how does he manage it? This is where the Illúvatar hypothesis seems most compelling. But if we take Tolkien at his word, that won't do.

Instead, I have another idea; it has to do with what Tom knows and how that informs his dominion. That is the subject of the next chapter.

---

22. Gollum, of course.

CHAPTER 3

"A LONG STRING OF NONSENSE-WORDS (OR SO THEY SEEMED)"

THE THING THAT delights many readers about Tom Bombadil is the thing that exasperates many others. I'm talking about Tom's nonsense singing. I suppose it's something of a Rorschach test. Your response to Tom's nonsense may say something about you.

Is the person who finds Tom irritating an artless person who drains life of its serendipity? Or, is the person who delights in Tom's nonsense some sort of flower child, traipsing through life with finger-paint on his hands? Or is this dichotomy the real nonsense?

Tom's singing isn't actually nonsense, although the rhymes may annoy you. (I enjoy them myself, but I have no pretense when it comes to taste—at least so far as poetry is concerned.) But I think that you need to read between the lines to see the sense in them.

Some people don't like reading between the lines because it strikes them as opening the door to all sorts of fanciful nonsense. They prefer plain language, and a direct and literal approach to interpretation. But is reading always so simple? Maybe life is art all the way down. And maybe when the original Artist said, "Let there be light,"

He had more than one thing in mind. Perhaps, just perhaps, the world doesn't read like the manual that came with your washing machine.

No matter, to the point here: Tolkien says that Tom's singing only *seemed* like nonsense. The line that tells us so is the title of this chapter.

The efficacy of Tom's singing is the best argument that it *isn't* nonsense. Tom's singing saves the hobbits more than once. And when we're first introduced to Tom, he tells the hobbits that it is his *songs* that will save them from Old Man Willow.

How do the songs work? We're not told. (And the hobbits never think to ask.) We do have clues to work with, but in order to see those clues we'll have to pan out a bit and look at the larger world in which *The Lord of the Rings* is set. But even more than this, we'll need to pan out still further to see the things that Tolkien thought are true in our world.

Knowledge is Power, Redux

Our first clue is Tom's lore. I'm using the old-fashioned word *lore* for "knowledge" in part because Tolkien does. But I'm also using it to contrast Tom's knowledge with what Saruman knows. Saruman knows things by breaking them. But what about Tom? We're told something about Tom's lore during the account of Tom's time with the hobbits over the course of a rainy day, "He...told them many remarkable stories...of bees and flowers, the ways of trees, and the strange creatures of the Forest," both the good and the bad when it came to them. Then we're told, "It was not comfortable lore." In particular he told them about, "the hearts of trees" and the bitter grudge they hold against creatures that can move about freely. To the trees they're all late-comers—nothing but usurpers, creatures who entered the world long after the trees.[1]

So, Tom knows things, good and bad things. But he doesn't seem to be interested in *using* what he knows, at least in the way Saruman does. Speaking of trees, it is worth recalling that later on, in another forest, two of the hobbits meet a distinctly tree-like person that actually walks and talks. For readers who have read the rest of the story, you know that I'm speaking of Treebeard. Treebeard is an ent, and ents are like shepherds, we're told, but instead of shepherding sheep, they shepherd trees. (And in Middle Earth, trees do need shepherds, if the episode with Old Man Willow tells us anything.)

Getting back to Saruman's way of knowing, Treebeard knows all about him because of his long history living near the wizard. What does Treebeard have to say about him? I quoted a portion of this before, now here's that quotation in context:

> 'But Saruman now!... I wonder now if even then Saruman was not turning to evil ways. But at any rate he used to give no trouble to his neighbours. I used to talk to him. There was a time when he was always walking about my woods. He was polite in those days, always asking my leave (at least when he met me); and always eager to listen. I told him many things that he would never have found out by himself; but he never repaid me in like kind. I cannot remember that he ever told me anything. And he got more and more like that; his face, as I remember it—I have not seen it for many a day—became like windows in a stone wall: windows with shutters inside.
>
> 'I think that I now understand what he is up to. He is plotting to become a Power. He has a mind of metal and

---

1. *The Fellowship of the Ring,* 127.

wheels; and he does not care for growing things, except as far as they serve him for the moment.'[2]

When it comes to what Tom and Treebeard know, they're open and generous. But Treebeard can't say the same for Saruman.

Treebeard now knows what Saruman was after with all his questions; he wanted power—power here meaning domination and use: "he does not care for growing things, except as far as they serve him for the moment." Intriguing, isn't it, how the pursuit of a particular form of knowledge closes you off from the world outside your head? Saruman's knowledge makes him machine-like, unfeeling and unaware of things outside himself. His knowledge is ignorant of the most important aspect of any given thing— what a thing is in itself. As a side note that may be of interest: etymologically the word *ignorant* actually means "on your own"—as we can see from the word *idiosyncrasy*. A person who shuts himself up like Saruman is ignorant in a very dangerous way, even though he knows many things.

Before you infer from this that Tolkien considered power evil in itself, remember that Tom is powerful—very powerful—in his own way. (The same could be said for Treebeard, or Gandalf, or Aragon, for that matter.) But Tom's power is based on a different kind of knowledge, and his knowledge is based on a different way of knowing.

Knowledge and Communion

You may be wondering if I'm making too much of this. If Tolkien were your typical writer, you'd be right to wonder. But that's not the sort of writer we're talking about here. We have some of his reflections on the matter in his essay

2. *The Two Towers*, 461–62.

"On Fairy Stories." Among the memorable things he says is that a genuine fairy story is generous in the way Bombadil and Treebeard are generous. The magic found in a fairy story is a magic that is intended to satisfy "certain primordial human desires. One of these desires is to survey the depths of space and time. Another is...to hold communion with other living things."[3]

Did you catch that? Communion is a goal, not control. This is why we can be fairly certain that if Saruman were to leap off the pages of *The Lord of the Rings* and take up residence in our world, he'd have no interest in fairy stories—not even the one he sprang from.

Saruman isn't interested in communion. He's a closed book—or as Treebeard put it—a stone wall with shuttered windows. You don't commune with things that you intend to use. Throughout *The Lord of the. Rings*, powerful characters who are good—Elrond, Gandalf, and Aragorn, among others—honor the free choices of those who are not as powerful as they are. And getting back to Treebeard, when Merry asks the Ent, "Would you think it rude, if we asked what you are going to do with us...?" the old Ent replies, "I am not going to do anything *with* you: not if you mean by that 'do something *to* you' without your leave. We might do some things together."[4] We can be sure that Saruman would not have been so considerate had he gotten his hands on Merry and Pippin—he would have done very unpleasant things to them in order to learn the whereabouts of the Ring of Power.

---

3. *Tree and Leaf*, 18.
4. *The Two Towers*, 455; italics in original.

Language and Power

Tolkien invented languages as a hobby. When I first learned this years ago I thought, "Well, to each his own, some people collect stamps." But even stamp collecting can reflect a deeper interest. And that's certainly the case with Tolkien and his languages. People in the know inform us that he didn't invent his stories first and then add languages later. Instead, first came the languages, then came the stories. First there was the Word, then came the world.

Words, when strung together in the right way, can stir us deeply, and even change us. They're magical in a sense. On the surface their meanings are derived from the world itself, but beneath the surface there is the Word—as in the *logos*—and this is the true source of all meaning, since the Word is what gives the world its form. Humans possess the power of speech, and in a limited sense, we can actually create meaning. But the meanings we make are derivative. We "subcreate," as Tolkien put it. And when we speak we cast spells. Think about the word *spell* for a moment. The sentences "She's a good speller; she won the spelling bee," and "She's a witch; she casts spells!" are getting at the magic of words. In his essay "On Fairy Stories," Tolkien said, "Small wonder that spell means both a story told, and a formula of power over living men."[5]

If stories cast a kind of spell, what sort of magic are we talking about? Well, two kinds: good magic and bad magic. If our spells are good, they're based on things that are true. If we're talking about bad magic—or black magic—then the words are woven so as to deceive people and contradict what it true.[6] They're lies. The most powerful lies are those that are the most deceptive, those that closely resemble

---

5. *Tree and Leaf,* 32.
6. Once again, see Tom Shippey, "New Learning and New Ignorance," in *Myth and Magic,* 22–46.

truth but actually conceal evil. And in *The Lord of the Rings* we see this with Saruman and his voice.

In *The Two Towers* (the second book of the trilogy), after the battle of Helm's Deep, Saruman is trapped in his tower by an army of angry Ents, and Gandalf and his companions pay him a visit. What follows is an enlightening encounter that illustrates the way speech can cast a kind of spell.

Gandalf warns his companions that they should be prepared for what they are about to hear.

> 'What's the danger?' asked Pippin. 'Will he shoot at us, and pour fire out of the windows; or can he put a spell on us from a distance?'
>
> 'The last is most likely, if you ride to his door with a light heart,' said Gandalf. 'But there is no knowing what he can do, or may choose to try.... And Saruman has powers you do not guess. Beware of his voice!'[7]

Later on the spells Saruman casts from a distance are described in this way:

> Suddenly another voice spoke, low and melodious, its very sound an enchantment. Those who listened unwarily to that voice could seldom report the words that they heard; and if they did, they wondered, for little power remained in them. Mostly they remembered only that it was a delight to hear the voice speaking, all that it said seemed wise and reasonable, and desire awoke in them by swift agreement to seem wise themselves. When others spoke they seemed harsh and uncouth by contrast; and if they gainsaid the voice, anger was kindled in the hearts of those under the spell. For some the spell lasted only while the voice spoke to them,.... For many the sound of the voice alone was enough to hold them enthralled; but for those whom it

---

7. *The Two Towers*, 562–63.

conquered the spell endured when they were far away, and
ever they heard that soft voice whispering and urging them.
But none were unmoved; none rejected its pleas and its
commands without an effort of mind and will, so long as
its master had control of it.[8]

What is Truth?

Seeing that there are both good spells and bad ones, how
can anyone tell the difference? As Gandalf asks, are we
wise enough to detect counterfeits?

To start with, we can subdivide the matter. There's truth
in the everyday, quotidian sense: "Tell the truth, Jimmy:
did you take a cookie from the cookie jar?" Then there is
truth in the largest sense—Truth with a capital—about
life, the universe, and the meaning of things. Any theory of
good spells must include both, but especially the latter. But
is there anything else that can be said about good spelling?

Tolkien gives a little glimpse of one way to tell the truth
with names when he has Treebeard describe Entish. The
language of the Ents is long and ponderous, reflecting the
age and the significance of the things they talk about. For
instance, when Treebeard finds Merry and Pippin he's
momentarily at a loss when it comes to the word they used
for the thing that the three of them are standing on.

'Let us leave this—did you say what you call it?'
'Hill?' suggested Pippin. 'Shelf? Step?' suggested
Merry.
Treebeard repeated the words thoughtfully. '*Hill*. Yes,
that was it. But it is a hasty word for a thing that has
stood here ever since this part of the world was shaped.'[9]

---

8. *The Two Towers*, 564.
9. *The Two Towers*, 455.

Treebeard implies here that names should reflect the histories of the things they name. Doing so not only tells you about those things; it also in some sense gives you power over them. This is why, when the hobbits introduce themselves to Treebeard, he is surprised by their rashness: "You call *yourselves* hobbits? But you should not go telling just anybody. You'll be letting out your own right names if you're not careful." They then tell him their names without hesitation. "'Hm, but you *are* hasty folk, I see,' said Treebeard. 'I am honoured by your confidence.'"[10]

Like Merry and Pippin you're probably puzzled by Treebeard's caution. That's probably because you share with them a modern view of language. In our time, names are not believed to be intimately connected to the things that they name; instead, they're believed to be arbitrary labels with no *real* relationship to the things themselves. But Treebeard doesn't subscribe to this understanding of language—he's too old for that.

Tolkien isn't just having fun here; he's actually describing an old way of thinking about the world. For instance, if you've ever wondered about the significance of names in the Bible, and *why* they are so significant, or why Isaac, after he learned that he had given his second-born (Jacob) the blessing intended for the first-born (Esau), couldn't just say, "Oops! I take it back," what you wondered about is this older understanding of words and their power.

The idea that true names and the things they refer to are somehow inseparable comes up in Tom's house. After a long day of tale telling, Frodo has the temerity to ask Tom the same question he asked Goldberry earlier.

'Who are you, Master?'...

---

10. *The Two Towers*, 454.

'Eh, what?' said Tom.... 'Don't you know my name
yet? That's the only answer. Tell me, who are you, alone,
yourself and nameless? But you are young and I am old.
Eldest, that's what I am. Mark my words, my friends:
Tom was here before the river and the trees; Tom remembers the first raindrop and the first acorn.'[11]

"Mark my words," Tom says; and why should they do
that? Because Tom's the "Eldest." Both Treebeard and Tom
can name things because of long experience with them.
That's explicitly stated by Treebeard, and implied here by
Tom. But Tom seems to be saying even more than that. He
tells the hobbits that he remembers the *beginning* of things.
And that's saying a lot, but it isn't the only suggestion that
we have that Tom knows more than Treebeard. The clue
that this is so is his nonsense singing—or as Tolkien puts
it, singing that *seemed* like nonsense.

The Nature of Music
and the Music of Nature

There's a lot of singing in *The Lord of the Rings*—in its
prequel, too (*The Hobbit*). What does this mean? I believe
more than is generally supposed; I think that it's a hint
about the nature of things in Middle Earth. But what's
being hinted at?

Let's begin with *The Hobbit*. There we have the deep
and stirring song of the dwarves as they sing about their lost
treasure in the evening shadows of Bag End; later we hear
the elves tease Bilbo, Gandalf, and the dwarves in song as
they descend into Rivendell. It seems like good creatures in
Middle Earth love to sing. Even wicked creatures sing, but
their songs have a wicked, sadistic character. The goblins

---

11. *The Fellowship of the Ring*, 129.

(like the Orcs of *The Lord of the Rings*), sing as they drive Bilbo and the dwarves through their tunnels beneath the Misty Mountains.

> *Clap! Snap! the black crack!*
> *Grip! grab! Pinch, nab!*
> *And down down to Goblin-town*
> *You go, my lad!*
>
> *Clash, crash! Crush, smash!*
> *Hammer and tongs! Knocker and gongs!*
> *Pound, pound, far underground!*
> *Ho, ho! my lad!*
>
> *Swish, smack! Whip crack!*
> *Batter and beat! Yammer and bleat!*
> *Work, work! Nor dare to shirk,*
> *While Goblins quaff, and Goblins laugh,*
> *Round and round far underground*
> *Below, my lad!*[12]

Tolkien adds, "The general meaning of the song was only too plain; for now the goblins took out whips and whipped them with a *swish, smack!*, and set them running as fast as they could in front of them."[13]

In *The Lord of the Rings* another wicked character sings—Old Man Willow. Tom tells the hobbits, "Old Grey Willow-man, he's a mighty singer; and it's hard for little folk to escape his cunning mazes."[14] While the Willow is as malicious as the goblins, their song merely described their glee as they torment Bilbo and the dwarves. But when it comes to Old Man Willow, not only are his songs bewitch-

---

12. *The Hobbit* (1937; New York: Houghton Mifflin, 1997), 56, 58.
13. *The Hobbit*, 58,
14. *The Fellowship of the Ring*, 124.

ing, they're hardly audible, and their general meaning isn't easy to discern.

All of this can be compared to and contrasted with the songs of Tom Bombadil. His songs have a peculiar *power*, and this is what I'd like to explore now.

But first let's take a little detour into a subject that might not seem like it has much to do with singing. Let's talk about Nature for a moment.

What we mean by the word "nature" is different today than the way it was once understood. Today nature is believed to be a single, self-contained thing. In antiquity, and the medieval world as well, people spoke of natures plural. For instance, in the old way of thinking you could actually speak of something called, "human nature" as distinct from the natures of other living things.[15]

Many people today blur distinctions between things in nature, arguing that these distinctions are not really Real, or permanent. For instance, we're told that human beings and orangutans share a remarkably high amount of DNA—over 97 percent—the implication being that there really isn't that much that separates people from apes.

But the blurring of distinctions goes even deeper than that. Humans and apes are said to still be evolving, and if that's so, we can't say anything conclusive about them. What's true today wasn't true once upon a time, and it may not be true tomorrow. This is one reason why we can't *truly* name things; we just name the impressions they make on us at the moment.

But it was once generally believed that the world as a whole, and the natures of things within it, reflected the wisdom of God. Paradoxically, the contemporary view has led to a revival of very ancient notions concerning how

---

15. For an in-depth analysis of the history of the word *nature*, see C. S. Lewis's *Studies in Words*.

things came to take the forms we see today. In pre-Christian ways of thinking, the world as we know it is the product of a violent process. Different myths tell different versions of the same story: one set of gods defeated another set of gods, and the world in which we find ourselves now is made up of the rotting corpses of the defeated. Things are not quite as colorful when it comes to the modern creation myths; that is because these new myths are about impersonal mechanisms. But the processes described are just as violent. As examples of what I mean, two contemporary theories which assert that violence is instrumental to human origins and the development of human society are Darwinism and Marxism.

But according to Tolkien's story, Middle Earth wasn't formed through a violent process. His world was made through creative intelligence from the Outside.

In *The Silmarillion*—Tolkien's posthumously published legendarium that informed both *The Hobbit* and *The Lord of the Rings*—we're given the story of that beginning. And there we learn that music played a key role in creation. Middle Earth is actually sung into being. Violent domination isn't the basis of its order; instead, the basis of order, and of being itself, is harmony. If you're not familiar with *The Silmarillion*, here's how the music is described in the first chapter.

In the beginning...

There was Eru, the One, who in Arda is called Illúvatar; and he made first the Ainur, the Holy Ones, that were the offspring of his thought, and they were with him before aught else was made. And he spoke to them, propounding to them themes of music; and they sang before him, and he was glad. But for a long while they sang only each alone, or but a few together, while the rest harkened; for each comprehended only that part of the mind of Illúvatar

from which he came, and in understanding of their breth-
ren they grew but slowly. Yet ever as they listened they
came to deeper understanding, and increased in unison
and harmony.[16]

What follows this is a grand chorus. And as the song
moves along, many themes run through it. But as the song
is sung, a singer named Melkor introduces disharmony to
the music, and some near him join in the dissonance. What
follows is a conflict that threatens to descend into chaos.
But Illúvatar introduces a new theme, and then another,
and saves the song and even enfolds the disharmony into
it. When the music is complete this follows:

> Then Illúvatar spoke, and he said: 'Mighty are the Ainur,
> and mightiest among them is Melkor; but that he may
> know, and all the Ainur, that I am Illúvatar, those things
> that ye have sung, I will show forth, that ye may see what
> ye have done.'[17]

Illúvatar then reveals that the song has become the flesh
and blood of a new world, the world in which *The Lord of
the Rings*, and every other story in Tolkien's legendarium,
is told.

Today many people rely on science to define Reality.
According to these folks, if science can't know something,
there's nothing to know. But science can't even explain its
own story scientifically. On the other hand, and on its own
terms, Christianity is the revelation of ultimate Reality.
And like Tolkien's Arda, according to the Christian faith,
the world that we live in was made from the Outside. In
Christianity, if anything is unnecessary it is the world. But

16. *The Silmarillion*, 2nd edition (1977; New York: Houghton Mifflin, 2001), 15.
17. *The Silmarillion*, 17.

what *is* necessary is the One who made it. Here's how the Apostle John put it in the introduction to his gospel:

> In the beginning was the Word, and the Word was with God, and the Word was God. He was in the beginning with God. All things were made through him, and without him was not any thing made that was made. (John 1:1-3)

This is one of the senses in which *The Lord of the Rings* is a fundamentally Catholic work—it is Catholic from the beginning.[18] The story that Tolkien wrote, with all of its strange creatures and imaginary people, is like our world; it was voiced into existence.

Perhaps you're beginning to see where this is leading: Bombadil's singing isn't nonsensical at all if it in some sense recalls the music of the Ainur.

"Eldest, that's what I am"

When you're old, you *should* know more than young folks. Since Tom is the oldest of all, he should know the most. And, by the way, Tom isn't the only person to say that he is incredibly old. Elrond does as well. At the Council of Elrond he said this:

> 'I had forgotten Bombadil, if indeed this is still the same that walked the woods and hills long ago, and even then was older than the old. That was not then his name. Iarwain Ben-adar we called him, oldest and fatherless.'[19]

In case you didn't know, Elrond is pretty old himself. When Frodo confesses his astonishment at the length of

---

18. There is some discussion as to whether by 'Catholic' Tolkien meant something close to what C.S. Lewis called, 'Mere Christianity' or something more in keeping with Roman Catholicism. I'll leave that to you to decide.
19. *The Fellowship of the Ring*, 258.

his memory, Elrond tells him, "My memory reaches back to the Elder Days.... I have seen three ages in the West of the world."[20] Three ages adds up to thousands of years, so when Elrond says someone is old, he's really old.

With these things in mind, a question occurred to me: is Tom old enough to remember the Song of the Ainur? If so, perhaps he knows the songs that gave created things their natures.

Adamic Language

We're told in Genesis that the animals were brought to Adam so that he could name them (Gen. 2:19). But how did he go about that? Did he just make up names arbitrarily, or did he base their names on something? If the latter, it must in some way express the natures of the things named. With this in mind, it was once believed that recovering Adamic language might help restore the dominion that was lost when Adam and Eve were expelled from Paradise.

One hypothesis was that Hebrew might be Adamic in nature; after all, the Old Testament was written in it. Another theory was that all human languages are some how adulterations of an original language. Philologists didn't get very far in their quest for that language though. Families of languages could be traced to common ancestors, Indo-European is the classic example—the mother tongue for many European tongues, Finnish and Basque being notable exceptions. But philology proved to be a dead end when it came to distilling an original Adamic language.

But odd as this may sound, there was another way back to an original primordial language, and that way was mathematics.

---

20. *The Fellowship of the Ring,* 237.

How can math give us a language with which to exercise dominion? Here's Galileo explaining how:

> Philosophy is written in this grand book, the universe, which stands continually open to our gaze. But the book cannot be understood unless one first learns to comprehend the language and read the letters in which it is composed. It is written in the language of mathematics, and its characters are triangles, circles, and other geometric figures without which it is humanly impossible to understand a single word of it; without these, one wanders about a dark labyrinth.[21]

The notion that you could use mathematics to understand the world may seem like a modern idea, but in fact it is a very old one. It is the way of the quadrivium, which is a branch of the liberal arts. And what this way was believed to lead you to may come as a surprise.

Classical education was something the Inklings understood well. (That honorary Inkling, Dorothy Sayers, actually wrote a book calling for its recovery, *The Lost Tools of Learning*.) It consisted of seven fields of study broken down into two groups—the trivium (for three), which followed this progression: grammar, logic, and rhetoric; and a second group, the quadrivium (for four) which followed another progression: arithmetic, geometry, astronomy, and (get this) *music*.

While the trivium focused on human language, the quadrivium was dedicated to the study of mathematics—the language of the physical world. The progression of the trivium is easy to follow. Grammar is the study of the structure of human language, logic is the structure of human reasoning, and rhetoric is a study of human

---

21. *The Assayer* (1623), translated by Stillman Drake in *Discoveries and Opinions of Galileo* (New York: Anchor Books, 1957), 237–38.

persuasion. The progress of the quadrivium is also easy to follow. First comes arithmetic, which could be called the grammar of numbers; then comes geometry, in which physical bodies are described with numbers; then astronomy, which today might go by the name physics, (or perhaps, cosmology), in which physical reality as a whole is mapped mathematically. So far so good, but what about music, the final art of the quadrivium? It seems like an odd thing to end this progression with; but actually, not so—not if you understand the elegant mathematical harmonies of the physical world.

The connection between mathematics and music goes back at least as far as Pythagoras, a name you may recall from his famous theorem. Pythagoras believed that numbers were the key to unlocking the secrets of Reality. But rather than making a materialist of him, mathematics made him a mystic. He thought that people should attune themselves to the grand music of the cosmos. In the old way of thinking, that music was known as the "Music of the Spheres." Essentially, someone who is attuned to the music of creation lives in harmony with all things.

Tolkien on Nature

As I conclude a chapter that has ambled on longer than I thought it would go, you may find yourself wondering if you're any further along in your understanding of the nature of Tom Bombadil's singing.

But there is one more thing to consider when it comes to Tom's songs. It's found in Tolkien's essay "On Fairy Stories." As he introduces the subject of fairies to us, he says this:

Supernatural is a dangerous and difficult word in any of its senses, looser or stricter. But to fairies it can hardly be applied, unless super is taken merely as a superlative prefix. For it is man who is, in contrast to fairies, super-natural (and often of diminutive stature); whereas they are natural, far more natural than he. Such is their doom.[22]

I take Tolkien here to mean that fairies in some sense belong to this world. Their natures are bound up with it. When it comes to Tom and Goldberry, there are subtle allusions to this—as when Galdor, pondering Tom's nature aloud at the Council of Elrond, says, "Power to defy our Enemy is not in him, unless such power is in the earth itself."[23] And when Frodo beholds Goldberry, delighting in the sound of her voice, we're told, "He stood as he had at times stood enchanted by fair elven-voices; but the spell that was now laid upon him was different: less keen and lofty was the delight, but deeper and nearer to mortal heart; marvelous and yet not strange."[24]

And this brings me back to the nature of good magic—or perhaps it would be better to say, the magic of nature. Throughout *The Lord of the Rings* good characters are puzzled by the term *magic* when referring to their crafts. One example of this can be heard in the conversation of the Lady Galadriel and Sam Gamgee at the Lady's mirror. Sam had said that he would like to have a glimpse of "Elf-magic," and now he gets his chance. She says to him:

> '[T]his is what your folk would call magic,...; though I do not understand clearly what they mean; and they seem also to use the same word of the deceits of the Enemy.'[25]

---

22. *Tree and Leaf*, 12.
23. *The Fellowship of the Ring*, 259. The Hebrew word for "soil" sounds like the name Adam. I'm sure that Tolkien knew this. Take that for what it is worth.
24. *The Fellowship of the Ring*, 121.
25. *The Fellowship of the Ring*, 353.

In some sense 'Elf-magic' works within given limits, because nature is a given, and in some sense not entirely subject to anyone's control. Good magic doesn't break things to know them, or pulverize them to repurpose them. Instead, it brings out latent goods in given things. We see it in the elven rope that Sam is given, or with lembas— the elven waybread—that the Fellowship is given (which is both delicious and sustaining), and especially with the elven cloaks they all receive that "magically" conceal their wearers, causing them to blend into the grass. Speaking of those cloaks, when the "three hunters"—Aragorn, Legolas, and Gimli—emerge from the grass when the Riders of Rohan nearly pass them by without seeing them, a rider says incredulously, "Do we walk in legends or on the green earth in the daylight?"

To this Aragorn replies, "The green earth, say you? That is a mighty matter of legend, though you tread it under the light of day!"[26]

Returning once more to the music of Ainur and Tom's songs, it's worth recalling that a song lies beneath the green grass of Rohan. And when it comes to the two branches of classical learning—the word-centered trivium and the number-centered quadrivium—when those branches come together, joining the inner life of the speaking mind to the mathematical harmonies of the given universe, the will of the speaker and the given Reality of creation can be harmonized. One does not have to obliterate the other, but instead there can be growth and fruitfulness. The dominion of the speaker is not a simple "Amen" to things as they are; and nature isn't merely a tyrant. Instead, creation leaves room for subcreation, and even elaboration—and a consummation of given things.

---

26. *The Two Towers*, 424.

With all of this in mind, perhaps, just perhaps, the reason Tom's songs seemed like nonsense to readers of *The Lord of the Rings* (and to the hobbits) is because Tom knows the music of the world, and we do not. And if that's so, then maybe what we think and say is the real nonsense.

CHAPTER 4

"FEAR NOTHING! FOR TONIGHT YOU ARE UNDER THE ROOF OF TOM BOMBADIL"

TOM IS MASTER, and his mastery has something to do with what he knows; but what difference does it make in the way he lives? It's when we're at home that we are truly ourselves. So, what does Tom's mastery look like when he is at home? In *The Lord of the Rings* we don't have to wait long to find out.

After their deliverance from Old Man Willow, the hobbits draw near to the house of Tom Bombadil.

They stumble out of the Forest and onto a lawn that swells before them. To one side, the headwaters of the Withywindle cascade over rocks, and run through a narrow channel as the water reflects the light of the stars just appearing in the evening sky. Then the reader is told:

> The grass under their feet was smooth and short, as if it had been mown or shaven. The eaves of the Forest behind were clipped, and trim as a hedge. The path was now plain before them,...[and] on a further slope, they saw the twinkling lights of a house. [1]

---

1. *The Fellowship of the Ring*, 119.

Then the door of the house opens and a bright beam flows out and soon they are welcomed into a haven of light and song.

Tom's house is a welcome respite from the perilous land that the hobbits have just passed through. And another peril is awaiting them on the farther side—the Barrow-downs. But between these perils—the Forest and the Downs—there is the House of Tom Bombadil.

Let's return to the root word we get the word *dominion* from: *domus*, Latin for "house." The title of this chapter is Goldberry's promise that under the roof of Tom Bombadil—under his dominion, in other words—there is no reason to fear.

We're told elsewhere that Tom's dominion includes the Old Forest as well as the Barrow-downs. But his house is different. There is a distinction between his domain and his domicile.

The Old Forest

When the hobbits originally entered the Old Forest they left the Shire behind them. The Shire is a well-tended garden, like the garden of the Lord. And it is in the west of Middle Earth, and the only place that we know much about that is farther west is the Grey Havens and the abode of Cirdan the Shipwright, the place of departure from Middle Earth to the Uttermost West. The Shire is walled in and protected by the Rangers of the North who patrol its borders and keep it safe without the knowledge of its inhabitants. Aragorn's kinsman Halbarad gives us a glimpse of their labors in this off-handed remark much later in the story: "A little people, but of great worth are the Shire-folk.... Little do they know of our long labour for the safekeeping of their borders, and yet I grudge it not."[2] Those labors have left their mark on the Rangers. Tending borders is dangerous work. Gimli, speaking to Legolas about the Rangers, says, "They are a strange company, these newcomers... Stout men and lordly they are, and the Riders of Rohan look almost as boys beside them; for they are grim men of face, worn like weathered rocks for the most part...and they are silent."[3]

The Old Forest is the first taste for the hobbits of what the world beyond the Shire has become. But that world wasn't always a fearful place. Tom speaks of a time, in the long past, even long before the coming of the kings from whom the Rangers descend, when the Forest was fearless. But it is fearful now, and passing through it is a sharp lesson for the hobbits. It is an unsettled place, inhospitable, a land for traveling through, not for dwelling in. It reminds me of the Land of Nod—the land of wandering—east of Eden, a place where people wander in search of rest but cannot find it. It's where Cain built his city—the prototype of every human city. And it is the land of Abraham's sojourning, which, paradoxically, according to the book of Hebrews, is the reason for his restlessness, because he sought a different city, a city whose builder is God himself.[4]

But it is right on the border of the Old Forest that Tom Bombadil has built his house. And this is an encouraging thought, since we find ourselves in a similar place. We live in a world that is like a wilderness. So perhaps there are some things to learn from Bombadil about living joyfully in our wilderness.

---

2. *The Return of the King,* 762.
3. *The Return of the King,* 759.
4. Hebrews 11:8-10. (The classic study of these cities is Augustine's *The City of God.*)

As the hobbits approach Tom's house, the first thing they notice is a contrast. They step out of a wild, unruly place into a carefully manicured space. The grass is closely trimmed, and even the Forest has been cut back like a hedge. Tom's no hippie. His home is well ordered and tame—it's domesticated.

Presumably even Tom needs a place to rest, and it is in his house that the hobbits find a home as comfortable and secure as any hobbit hole, actually more so, because Tom is there. He is their shelter. If he were *not* there, would his house be a haven from "tree-shadows" or "untame things" as Goldberry assures them is the case when they are under his roof? He's indomitable; he's the Master. What they enjoy at this point in the story is his domicile, a house that suits him and his wife. And it suits the hobbits, too. In his house they find basins and ewers filled with cold or steaming water, soft green slippers, and comfortable mattresses with pillows that are soft as down and blankets that are white as wool.

Stories and Candles

After their first night in Tom's house, the hobbits awaken from dreams both portentous and disturbing to the happy fortune of a rainy day. Tom tells them that it's Goldberry's washing day, and travel is impossible. So candles are lit, the fire in the hearth is tended, and Tom regales the hobbits with stories—stories about everything from the fall of the trees from lordship into the darkness of resentment, to the queer ways of badgers; from the rise and fall of small kingdoms, to the coming of hobbits to the West; of the first raindrop and the first acorn when the dark was not fearsome; to the coming of the Dark Lord from Outside.

My friend Rachel Fulton Brown, a medievalist at the University of Chicago, believes that Goldberry's washing day serves as the baptism of the hobbits into the grand story of Middle Earth. She notes that stories are told at turning points in *The Lord of the Rings*, and in the end, Sam and Frodo—and especially Sam—remind themselves when all seems lost, at least for them—that they have played a part in the great story of the world. Here's that moving scene right after Sam recalls the story of Beren and his quest to retrieve a Silmaril from the crown of Morgoth:

'Why, to think of it, we're in the same tale still! It's going on. Don't the great tales never end?'

'No, they never end as tales,' said Frodo. 'But the people in them come, and go when their part's ended. Our part will end later—or sooner.'

'And then we can have some rest and some sleep,' said Sam. He laughed grimly. 'And I mean just that, Mr. Frodo. I mean plain ordinary rest, and sleep, and waking up to a morning's work in the garden. I'm afraid that's all I'm hoping for all the time. All the big important plans are not for my sort. Still, I wonder if we shall ever be put into songs or tales. We're in one, of course; but I mean: put into words, you know, told by the fireside, or read out of a great big book with red and black letters, years and years afterwards. And people will say: "Let's hear about Frodo and the Ring!"'[5]

But here, at the beginning of their story, Rachel thinks that the hobbits receive their catechesis. I find her insight compelling, especially in light of how in the journey to come, significant events correspond to dates in the Christian liturgical calendar.[6] Here, in Tom's house then, we

5. *The Two Towers*, 697.
6. For example, Sauron is defeated on March 25th—which in the Christian liturgical calendar is the Feast of the Annunciation, also known as the Feast of the Incarnation, which commemorates the visit of the Archangel Gabriel to the

hear the Grand Story of the world, the world where every story finds its place.

But great writers can do more than one thing at a time. And I think that Tolkien is doing that here—I think he's also telling us something about the nature of good households and how they fit into the Grand Story.

The Harmony of Tom and Goldberry

A beautiful harmony can be sensed in Tom's house. We see it in the mundane, the earthy routines of Tom and Goldberry. Even when Tom's not singing, his words have a lyrical quality. And Goldberry's movements as she lights candles or tends the table are as graceful as a dance. When they speak or move in concert, there seems to be music that only they can hear.

And even though Tom and Goldberry seem to embody different themes, . . .

> Yet in some fashion they seemed to weave a single dance, neither hindering the other, in and out of the room, and round about the table; and with great speed food and vessels and lights were set in order.[7]

And once their preparations are complete, in a blink, without explanation or observation, they appear before the hobbits in formalwear, dressed for the evening meal. Then begins a jolly time, and before long the hobbits have apparently picked up the tune. After drinking what appears to be nothing more than water, the hobbits are "singing merrily"—as though singing was "more natural than talking."[8]

Virgin Mary.
7. *The Fellowship of the Ring*, 129.
8. *The Fellowship of the Ring*, 123.

"More natural than talking"—that's a telling way of putting it. Here's a little inside information: in Tolkien's legendarium we learn that the music of the Ainur can most readily be heard in the waters of Middle Earth.[9]

Communion: Natures in Harmony

Natures living in harmony is something that many of our ancestors would have recognized on sight but which requires a word of explanation today. Tom and Goldberry's dance about the table, setting dishes and lighting candles, says something. Their movements are not unreflective and spontaneous—they're artful, reflecting creative intent. And those actions are set within a world made with creative intent. They are participating in something grand, something larger than themselves.

If our world is also a work of art, then why can't we hear music ringing in our ears the way that Tom and Goldberry seem to? Could it have something to do with how we perceive things? Are we even listening? Do we want to? We live in a tone-deaf time and we behave as though there's no natural order to harmonize with; instead, we think that the world should just do what we tell it to do. Naturally, if that is all there is to it, then freedom is nothing more than doing what you want to do, and laws and customs can be boiled down to some people bossing other people around. The suspicion that this is all there is to it now runs so deep in our time that even marriage as the happy harmony of a man and wife has been lost. It has

9. J.R.R. Tolkien, *Morgoth's Ring* (London: HarperCollins, 2015), 12–13. In the same book we're told: "But Ulmo was alone, and he abode not in Valinor, but dwelt from the beginning of Arda in the Outer Ocean, as he still does; and thence he governed the flowing of all waters, and the courses of all rivers, the replenishment of springs and the distilling of rain and dew throughout the world. In the deep places he gives thought to music great and terrible; and the echo thereof runs through all the veins of the earth" (20).

been "deconstructed" in the interest of "liberation" and what we see in Tom and Goldberry is more the exception than the rule today.

But if Tolkien is saying something true about our world with his imaginary world, then the music is still playing in our world, and what we need in our time is our hearing restored.

Paradise Lost

But even in Middle-Earth it is possible to get so lost in your own tune that you no longer hear anything else. That's not true for Tom and Goldberry—each sings the praise of the other because it is not only singing but listening that makes for harmony. Unfortunately the same can't be said for the Ents and their wives.

One of the oddities of Fangorn—the forest where Treebeard lives—is its thoroughgoing masculinity. All the Ents who live there are male, and even the forest itself seems to have a male cast of mind. (I'll say why in a moment.) It isn't as though female Ents don't exist—or didn't exist. It's just that they're not to be found in the wild. Where *do* they live? No one can say. But we learn from Treebeard what sort of place they would be found in if the Ents could ever find their wives. It would be a place very much like the Shire where the hobbits are from—a small and cultivated land, full of things that are planned and tended, a place that has been thoroughly domesticated and made to serve, a place remarkably like a large house.

Here's a snatch of monologue from Treebeard as he ruminates on the differences between the Ents and the Entwives:

'It is a rather strange and sad story,' he went on after a pause. 'When the world was young, and the woods were wide and wild, the Ents and the Entwives—and there were Entmaidens then: ah! the loveliness of Fimbrethil, of Wandlimb the lightfooted, in the days of our youth!—they walked together and they housed together. But our hearts did not go on growing in the same way: the Ents gave their love to things that they met in the world, and the Entwives gave their thought to other things, for the Ents loved the great trees, and the wild woods, and the slopes of the high hills; and they drank of the mountain-streams, and only ate such fruit as the trees let fall in their path; and they learned of the Elves and spoke with the Trees. But the Entwives gave their minds to the lesser trees, and to the meads in the sunshine beyond the feet of the forests; and they saw the sloe in the thicket, and the wild apple and the cherry blossoming in spring, and the green herbs in the waterlands in summer, and the seeding grasses in the autumn fields. They did not desire to speak with these things; but they wished them to hear and obey what was said to them. The Entwives ordered them to grow according to their wishes, and bear leaf and fruit to their liking; for the Entwives desired order, and plenty, and peace (by which they meant that things should remain where they had set them). So the Entwives made gardens to live in. But we Ents went on wandering, and we only came to the gardens now and again.'[10]

I think it is a mistake to think of dominion entirely in terms of good and bad. Instead I believe it is better to think of it as coming in two keys: rule and cultivation. The Ents care for the world as they find it in itself. They love large and wild things, things that they rule only in the interest of the things as they are found in themselves. I suppose this could be called "wildlife management," although I prefer "rule" to management. (Managers never give up control;

---

10. *The Two Towers*, 464–65.

rulers intervene only when some rule has been violated—as we see with Tom and Old Man Willow.) I think that this is the space within a dominion in which freedom is given room—it is the open space in which wolves hunt, boys play with pocket-knives, and businesses get started. (As you may know, all these things are endangered in our world because of an over-emphasis on safety and equality.)

But where would we be without gardens? Tom has one. When the hobbits enter Tom's house, they come in from the wild outside to an ordered and peaceful place filled with good things. It's the sort of place that Entwives would have felt at home in (if they could be made to fit!). Tom's house is dominion in another key, a place of things ordered to serve.

Naming the Elephant

It is impossible to move on without at least acknowledging the question you've probably asked yourself. Here it is: Is dominion good for the environment? There, the elephant in the room has been named. So, what about it?

Many influential people believe that the biblical doctrine of dominion is behind climate change and the extinction of species, and a myriad of other regrettable things.[11] But the problem with this view is that dominion is a fact—human beings simply have it. It's God's doing. We can't abdicate. Human beings possess power over all the creatures of the world. I suppose you could say we have a Ring of Power—whether we want it or not.

But dominion isn't arbitrary power, at least not originally. In the Christian faith human dominion is subject to

---

11. Notably, Lynn White, Jr. in "The Historical Roots of Our Ecological Crisis," *Science* 155 (March 1967): 1203-7.

God's dominion. And it is informed by God's Law—his moral standard, his holiness. We can't just do as we please.

So how should we go about exercising the dominion that we have been given? Well, I think that Tom is more helpful than Treebeard here. Tom can sing the tune of dominion in two keys (rule and cultivation). We must make a place for ourselves in the world, a place where we have ordered things to our liking. But that isn't everything. And that doesn't mean we've abdicated office when we leave things alone. It can just mean that we rule those things in the interest of those things—to the glory of their Maker.

Discarded Images

C. S. Lewis described an image of the cosmos that has been discarded by modern people in his last book, aptly titled *The Discarded Image*. In the old image we were surrounded by translucent spheres that rotated musically around us. Our home in this image is at the bottom—which is also the center. Even though it is the scene of a great drama, it's a small thing, a speck of dense material enveloped by vast regions of light. But even though the scale of the image is vast, it was still small enough for people to contemplate. You could discern its working in the sky right overhead. And you could see its limit when you looked up at the fixed stars of the outermost sphere.

We see something like this old image in Tolkien's legendarium. The stars of Middle Earth are not merely named for people—some of them *are* people.[12] In the old image the cosmos was large enough to encourage humility, but not so large as to make you feel meaningless. We see this when Frodo and Sam are in Mordor; Sam looks

---

12. Earendil the Mariner, for instance. We see something similar in C. S. Lewis's *Voyage of the Dawn Treader*.

up and sees the stars, and he finds comfort in the thought that even the Dark Lord is a small thing when compared to the vast expanse above.

> Sam struggled with his own weariness...and there he sat silent till deep night fell. Then at last, to keep himself awake, he crawled from the hiding-place and looked out... Far above the Ephel Dúath in the West the night-sky was still dim and pale. There, peeping among the cloud-wrack above a dark tor high up in the mountains, Sam saw a white star twinkle for a while. The beauty of it smote his heart, as he looked up out of the forsaken land, and hope returned to him. For like a shaft, clear and cold, the thought pierced him that in the end the Shadow was only a small and passing thing: there was light and high beauty for ever beyond its reach.[13]

Today, with the help of telescopes and other instruments, we know that the cosmos is far larger than our ancestors could have imagined. The logical inference seems clear enough: it can't all be just for us.

So, what's it all for if it isn't for us? It isn't as though the Bible fails to address this. In the Bible we see God riding upon the storm and speaking from the whirlwind. And when the psalmist asks, "What is man that you are mindful of him?" (Psalm 8:4) we can hear the question if we read between the lines. According to the Bible, creation is a very capacious place—and most of it is beyond our reach, at least for the moment. That's worth keeping in mind, not only because it puts the evils of our world in proper perspective, but also because it tempers our ambitions.

But with the way we think of the cosmos today, we can taste a bitter irony. The limits of the universe have so receded from view; there seems to be no place for human

---

13. *The Return of the King*, 901.

beings anymore. Man's subcreative powers are now believed to be an anomaly, even a blight, a kind of virus spreading through the system. The moral imperative is now to become even smaller than we already are, perhaps even to disappear entirely for the good of the environment.

Perhaps Tom can help us here. Maybe the ridiculous fellow in the bright blue jacket and yellow boots can teach us to sing the song of dominion in two keys—the keys of rule and cultivation. Perhaps dominion should be understood to mean ordering some things for our good, and other things for the good of those things in themselves. If that's so—and I think that it is—we will not only let elephants run wild, we will commune with them at the same time.

CHAPTER 5

"GOLDBERRY IS WAITING"

I DOUBT THAT this chapter will satisfy some of my readers. My excuse, if I may be excused, is I just don't have as much to work with as I'd like. If Tom is an enigma, what can we hope to say about Goldberry? She seems twice removed. Would traveling twice as far bring us any closer to her? Any shooter will tell you that the farther away you are from the target, the degree of error is magnified. A shot that hits the bull's-eye at twenty feet may miss the target entirely at two hundred.

Yet there is material to work with, a few hints, and telling actions—especially on Tom's part. But I think I will need to call in help from outside the story once again. My leaping-off point is this: Tom called her "the River-woman's Daughter."

The River-Woman's Daughter

Tom is fatherless; Elrond tells us so. But Goldberry is the River daughter. I think that implies at least that she is the younger of the two—and Tom does call her "young Goldberry" at least once. While Tom's nature may be bound up with the *earth*, Goldberry is certainly tied to

water, particularly the Withywindle.[1] So it seems that Tom
and Goldberry complement each other in an elemental
way.[2] They live at the head of the river, and we never see
her far from it. Rivers may meander, and their banks erode,
and they can swell with rain, and dwindle in drought, but
more or less they say put. Apparently the same can be said
of Goldberry.

Let's take a look at a few references to Goldberry and
water in the story.

To begin with, we hear this when we first meet Tom.
He's bringing something home for her.

> *Hey! Come merry dol! derry dol! My darling!*
> *Light goes the weather-wind and the feathered starling.*
> *Down along under Hill, shining in the sunlight,*
> *Waiting on the doorstep for the cold starlight,*
> *There my pretty lady is, River-woman's daughter,*
> *Slender as the willow-wand, clearer than the water.*
> *Old Tom Bombadil water-lilies bringing*
> *Comes hopping home again. Can you hear him singing?*[3]

---

1. "'I know little of Iarwain save the name,' said Galdor; 'but Glorfindel, I think, is
right. Power to defy our Enemy is not in him, unless such power is in the earth
itself'" (*Fellowship of the Ring*, 259; Iarwain is an Elvish name for Bombadil).
One last note is worth making here. In *The History of Middle-earth*, volume 10,
Morgoth's Ring, after *The Lord of the Rings* had been published, Tolkien wrote
this: "Outside the Blessed Realm, all 'matter' was likely to have a 'Melkor ingre-
dient'...in this way Morgoth lost (or exchanged, or transmuted) the greater part
of his original 'angelic' powers, of mind and spirit, while gaining a terrible grip
upon the physical world.... Morgoth's vast power was disseminated. The whole of
'Middle Earth' was Morgoth's Ring" (400). I would have made more of this in this
book if I could prove that the Good Professor had this in mind when he inserted
Tom into *The Lord of the Rings*. But I think that if he had a sense of this when he
wrote about Tom, especially considering Tom could remember a time before the
coming of the Dark Lord from the Outside, Tom would then embody the original
intent of Eru (aka, Illúvatar), and what was lost for both Elves and Men—Illúvatar's Children—and their lost dominion. If that's so, Tom represents Middle Earth
untainted—aka, unfallen.
2. In antiquity it was believed that there were only four elements: earth, water,
air, and fire. Here we have two perhaps represented: Tom—earth, and Goldberry—water.
3. *The Fellowship of the Ring*, 117.

This may be a bit like bringing roses home to your wife on Valentine's Day, but I'm not certain that I understand even that as well as I should. Perhaps we have something here that gets at the nature of things feminine, and not just Goldberry in particular.

Water, Spirits, and Women

We see something along this line in Taoism, with the Yin and Yang apposition—female as wet and cool, and male as dry and hot. And throughout the world the association of a feminine spirit with small bodies of water—streams, ponds, even rivers—seems typical and not merely coincidental. But perhaps this is saying too much; still Goldberry goes with the Withywindle, and the Withywindle goes with her. When the hobbits get to Tom's house they actually come to its headwaters.

> Just as they felt their feet slowing down to a standstill, they noticed that the ground was gently rising. The water began to murmur. In the darkness they caught the white glimmer of foam, where the river flowed over a short fall.... The river, now small and swift, was leaping merrily down to meet them, glinting here and there in the light of the stars, which were already shining in the sky.[4]

And when Goldberry's voice is first heard here is how it is described:

> Then another clear voice,...like the song of glad water flowing down into the night from a bright morning in the hills, came falling like a silver to meet them:

---

4. *The Fellowship of the Ring,* 119.

Now let the song begin! Let us sing together
Of sun, stars, moon and mist, rain and cloudy weather,
Light on the budding leaf, dew on the feather,
Wind on the open hill, bells on the heather,
Reeds by the shady pool, lilies on the water:
Old Tom Bombadil and the River-daughter![5]

This is delightful, at least I think so, but it is also a little odd. If you have the good fortune to have access to Carol Rose's *Spirits, Fairies, Leprechauns, and Goblins: An Encyclopedia,* you'll likely notice that spirits associated with water are often malignant creatures, or at least ambiguous ones. And sometimes they are hideous. One example is Jenny Greenteeth, who was a water spirit believed to dwell in small ponds in the northeast of England. She hid beneath the surface, waiting for unwary children to venture too close; then she'd emerge and grab a hapless child in her long green fangs and pull him under to drown.[6]

It was while I pondered the incongruity of Jenny and Goldberry, and turning the pages of Rose's encyclopedia, that I came across this entry—

BÜT IAN ÜDERŽƏ

This is the name of a water spirit in the folklore of the Cheremis/Mari people of the former Soviet Republic. The BÜT IAN ÜDERŽƏ, which means Water Devil's Daughter, is a female fresh water spirit of human shape. This spirit is subordinate to the main spirit venerated for a stretch of water and is therefore called the "daughter" of that spirit, in this case Büt Ian. Büt Ian Üderžə may sometimes be seen on a river bank combing her long golden hair with a gold or silver comb. Mortal men may

5. *The Fellowship of the Ring,* 119–120.
6. Carol Rose, *Spirits, Fairies, Leprechauns, and Goblins: An Encyclopedia* (New York: W.W. Norton and Company, 1998), 167.

be able to marry her if they can catch her, by touching her with iron, which renders her unable to escape. However, if the true identity of the spirit is ever revealed, she will die like a mortal immediately.[7]

Certain features of *Büt Ian Üderžə* remind me of Goldberry—and the similarities seem too great to be coincidental. There are obvious ones—both are water spirits, and both have long golden hair. But more telling was the matter of being a "daughter." Yet above all there's the way that she can be made your wife—specifically that a man may marry her if he can catch her. The reason that's so telling isn't because of anything we're told in *The Lord of the Rings*; it's because of something we learn in "The Adventures of Tom Bombadil," a poem about Tom found in a collection of poems published under the same title.

That poem takes up the theme "No one has ever caught old Tom yet!" There's a familiar cast of characters, and each does his best to catch him. There's Old Man Willow, the Barrow wight, and even a Badger brock. But the first to try, believe it or not, is Goldberry. In the poem Tom is sitting by the Withywindle when this happens:

> *There his beard dangled long down into the water:*
> *up came Goldberry, the River-woman's daughter;*
> *pulled Tom's hanging hair, in he went a-wallowing*
> *under the water-lilies, bubbling and a-swallowing.*[8]

Now here's something that we'd expect of Jenny Green-teeth. But unlike Old Man Willow, the Badger brock, or the Barrow wight, Goldberry's attempt to trap Tom strikes me as flirtatious. She takes his feathered hat and asks him,

---

7. Rose, 56.
8. *A Tolkien Miscellany* (Quality Paperback Club, 2002), 169.

"Hey, Tom Bombadil! Whither are you going?"[9] I can't help hearing an undertone of romantic interest here. Tom's retort seems to say that the attraction is mutual, but he's not about to live with her on her terms:

> 'You bring it back again, there's a pretty maiden!'
> said Tom Bombadil. 'I do not care for wading.
> Go down! Sleep again where the pools are shady
> far below the willow-roots, little water-lady!'
> Back to her mother's house in the deepest hollow
> swam young Goldberry. But Tom, he would not follow.[10]

The mystery of romantic love is profound, and it does not accord with the democratic temper of our time. In it there is passion and pursuit, fear and flight. Reducing it to a contract between equals drains it of its power. Our ancestors played in pools too deep for us. Deracinated and inter-changeable genders may keep the corporate flow-charts flipping, but the un-sexed don't know how to play hide-and-seek with the opposite sex. That's why the happy ending of this poem is lost on us, because it ends when Tom catches Goldberry. And this is a beautiful thing.

> But one day Tom, he went and caught the River-daughter,
> in green gown, flowing hair, sitting in the rushes,
> singing old water-songs to birds upon the bushes.
> He caught her, held her fast! Water-rats went scuttering
> reeds hissed, herons cried, and her heart was fluttering.
> Said Tom Bombadil: "Here's my pretty maiden!
> You shall come home with me! The table is all laden:
> yellow cream, honeycomb, white bread and butter;
> roses at the window-sill and peeping round the shutter.

9. A Tolkien Miscellany, 169.
10. A Tolkien Miscellany, 169.

You shall come under Hill! Never mind your mother
in her deep weedy pool: there you'll find no lover!"[11]

Pursuit and capture, it's a dangerous game—and it can go wrong in many ways. But there's no mystery to missing the mark; instead, the mystery is hidden in hitting it. It is when the heart flutters in the capturing embrace that catching and being caught amount to the same thing. And if you don't understand that I'm afraid that I cannot help you.

For a man, a house without a wife is a cold and sterile thing. In ages of the world when the wilderness was just beyond the hedge, that was obvious. A man can live alone, but not fruitfully. It's in the nature of things, for a husband and wife bring a good return. In our time we've lost our sense of the nature of things—particularly the fruitfulness of a home where women and the feminine arts are honored.

Which brings me back to the title of this chapter, "Goldberry is waiting." We hear this for the first time when we meet Tom going home again, water-lilies bringing. But it isn't the last time. What the water-lilies are for, Tom doesn't say. But then we see them in use when we first meet Goldberry.

When the hobbits arrive she's seated at home, long yellow hair "rippling down," and she is dressed almost entirely in green, the green of her gown as "green as young reeds," yet accented with silver, "like beads of dew." Surrounding her, in large clay vessels filled with water, are the water lilies Tom brought her, now floating, creating the impression that Goldberry is the midst of a pool. Here in Bombadil's house she is revealed to be someone with authority and, as Tolkien writes, she "seemed to be enthroned."[12]

Seemed? Tolkien seems to use that word a lot, especially when speaking of Tom or Goldberry. But seeming can amount to being if you believe that appearances can sometimes tell the truth. I think here the cord between the sign and what it signifies can't be cut. Tom honors Goldberry, and acknowledges her nature. She is enthroned in the house of Tom Bombadil. He is the Master of his house, as he is the Master of "wood, water, and hill."[13] And as with those things, his mastery does not amount to ownership—Goldberry belongs to herself, and yet he's caught her. She is his wife: truths can layer and not displace each other. In a flat world things grow in significance at the expense of other things, but in a vertically ordered world, things can freely be themselves, even when they are subject to others. Mastery does not equal ownership—even when people are subject to you.

Goldberry's Washing Day

Goldberry's place in the order of things outside the house is not entirely clear, but we do have clues. And one of them I've already mentioned—Goldberry's washing day.

The making and the care of clothing has been women's work in many traditional cultures throughout the world. And this has included washing days when groups of women trudged down to the nearest stream to scrub and beat dirty clothes clean. But when it comes to folklore, seeing a fairy washer woman was often a bad sign. An example is *Ban Nighechain*; here's how she's described by Carol Rose in her encyclopedia:

---

12. *The Fellowship of the Ring*, 121.
13. *The Fellowship of the Ring*, 122.

In Celtic Scottish folk lore Ban Nighechain, whose name
means Little Washer Woman, is a female spirit of forebod-
ing and doom. She is also known as Nigheag na H-ath,
which means Little Washer of the Ford. She is described
as a little old woman with only one nostril, protruding
teeth, and red webbed feet. The Ban Nighechain is seen
standing in the ford of a river, washing the blood-soaked
clothes of the dying taken from battle. Death or disaster
are imminent for anyone she sees.[14]

And that's just one example; Rose cites several others.
I cannot say if Tolkien had these fay in mind when he
describes Goldberry's washing day, but she makes for
quite a contrast nonetheless.

In the morning following their first night at Tom's
house, the hobbits look out of the windows and see rain
clouds rolling in. The turn in the weather keeps them from
resuming their journey, and the day that they spend with
Tom is instructive in many ways. But for the better part
of the day Goldberry isn't seen. She's busy, we're told. It's
her washing day. What seems to be a domestic chore, we
discover actually serves something much larger.

> As [the hobbits] looked out of the window there came
> falling gently as if it was flowing down the rain out of the
> sky, the clear voice of Goldberry singing up above them.
> They could hear few words, but it seemed plain to them
> that the song was a rain-song, as sweet as showers on dry
> hills, that told the tale of a river from the spring in the
> highlands to the Sea far below.[15]

Goldberry doesn't appear again until evening, just
as Tom mentions the coming of "the Dark Lord...from
Outside." Then, at that point, something dark goes by a

14. Rose, 32.
15. *The Fellowship of the Ring*, 127.

window. The hobbits look out, then in the doorway behind them, she appears, bearing a candle, and she is "framed in light"—light even radiating through the hand she holds before the flame. She then announces that the rain has ended, implying that her washing day is done. And with that she says, "Let us now laugh and be glad!"[16]

What could it all mean? Here are a few cautious suggestions. When it comes to the rain, what isn't at all clear is what's the cause and what's the effect. Perhaps that's a wrong-headed way of putting it. We tend to think of things causing each other directly: does her singing bring the rain? Does it bless the rain? Does it direct the rain? Does it just accompany it, as though the rain is its inspiration? Perhaps it interprets the rain? Who can say? Does it matter? The rain, and the song, and Goldberry all go together.

Jenny Greenteeth wasn't beautiful; that's because she reflected a dark undercurrent of the minds of people who live by rivers and ponds: water brings death as well as life. Recall, in "The Adventures of Tom Bombadil," Goldberry pulled Tom underwater, just like malicious water spirits found in the folklore. Most hobbits don't like boats, and they don't like rivers. (Both are tricky.)[17] Rivers nourish life because they water the things that live along their banks, but they can also kill those who fall into them. And then there is the sea, a super-abundance of water, teeming with life, but if it breaches its boundaries it can wash the land clean of life and leave dead things littered everywhere.[18]

---

16. *The Fellowship of the Ring*, 129.

17. This made hobbits outside Buckland suspicious of Bucklanders (a branch of the extended hobbit family) because they lived on the "wrong side" of the Brandywine River and used boats. And Frodo's parents were said to have drowned in the river—see the Gaffer's account in "A Long-expected Party," in *The Fellowship of the Ring*.

18. For your information, Tolkien was a translator of the book of Jonah for the Jerusalem Bible, so it is safe to say that he was familiar with the ambiguous nature of water as it is understood in the Bible.

Water must be measured out in the right amount if it is to bring life instead of death. Does this tell us anything about Goldberry? And, by implication, does it say anything about Tom?

Baptizing the Pagan Imagination

It's important to say up front that what I have to say may not have been Tolkien's intent when he created Goldberry. But whether it was or not, Tolkien seems to have redeemed a water fay, and I suppose that means Tom did, too.

Think about it this way—Goldberry is the River woman's daughter, and Tom caught her and brought her home. Goldberry has been domesticated.

When we consider the natural world without some redeeming framework to appraise it, its ambiguity both attracts and horrifies us. On a sunny day, from the safe remove of my porch, I look across a road to the field beside my house, and I am delighted. The calls of the birds, the light breeze that makes leaves flit and flash, the birches that bend gracefully against a white-laced sky in the distance—these things please me. Yet in the small pond in the middle of that field, in its muddy depths, there are creatures swallowing each other whole; and a small child wandering that field alone could fall in. (I knew a man who lost a child in that very way in a different pond.) And you don't need a pond for death to show his face in the field near my house. The coyotes and hawks I've seen there many times can do that. They ever roam and soar, seeking something to devour. So, whenever we look outdoors, we see beauty and death in the same face called Nature. Can the same be said for Goldberry?

One of my daughters-in-law, puzzling aloud about Goldberry, asked me, "What is Goldberry good for? Is she some sort of trophy-wife?" As I've thought about it, my qualified answer is yes, but perhaps she's a dangerous one.

In the history of Christianity, missionaries have tended to follow one of two broad strategies when it comes to evangelizing pagan cultures. One is what I call the "scorched-earth method," and the other is the "fulfillment method."

When it comes to the scorched-earth method, like Sherman's march to the sea, anything that may encourage pagan notions or sentiments is consigned to the flames. The campaign to purify is predicated on the notion that any taint of pagan provenance ruins all. It is also assumed that the Christian faith can be introduced whole, a brand new thing coming down from above like the New Jerusalem. There are many problems with this. One of them is the problem of language. Take the word *pagan*, for instance—it's a pagan word. It isn't found in the Bible. It's Latin. It originally meant something like "rustic" or "countrified." In other words, it's a word that Christians adopted and repurposed to mean "non-Christian." (How that happened is a story in itself.) Language grows in the soil of a culture, and as Tolkien maintained, it is bound up inextricably with the stories that people make up to understand themselves and the world. Since this is so, the only way a culture could be purified is by burning its vocabulary to the ground and introducing an entirely new language. But is such a thing even possible, let alone desirable?

The word *redemption* seems to imply something different. For something to be redeemed in at least one sense, it must remain what it is. What that implies is that it must have enough intrinsic value to make it worth redeeming in the first place.

Is there anything intrinsically valuable when it comes to the folklore surrounding water spirits? Is there something worth redeeming? I think so, and I think that Tolkien and his friend C. S. Lewis were particularly gifted at finding value in pagan stories. Take Lewis's story *The Lion, the Witch, and the Wardrobe*. There we are introduced to a little satyr named Mr. Tumnus. He's a remarkable person. For one thing he resembles Pan, a god in Greek mythology associated with sexuality and licentiousness. Like Pan, he has a human torso and head, but his nether-parts are those of a goat (implying the sexual proclivities of a goat). But Lewis wisely refers to him with the Latin *faun*, perhaps because calling him a satyr would have had people reaching for their encyclopedias, where they would learn about bacchanalia and all that.

But Lewis does more than just tame the image with a name; he gives his satyr the civilizing accessories of a package and an umbrella. He might as well have been an accountant waiting for the omnibus. But Mr. Tumnus is still a dangerous creature, as a young girl named Lucy discovers after he tries to enchant her with his pipes so that he can hand her over to the White Witch. Mr. Tumnus doesn't go through with his scheme because Lewis has also given him something of a Christian conscience. And before the end Mr. Tumnus has asked for Lucy's forgiveness. Through the episode we see both the charm and the danger of the original satyr, but the danger, while still present, is sublimated and, in a subtle way, repurposed.

And this is what I believe we can see in Goldberry. There's no doubt that Tolkien was fully aware of the danger, and even the malice, in the folklore of water spirits. Whether or not Tolkien intentionally set out to convert a Jenny Greenteeth, who can say? But it doesn't really matter. Anyone who has ever written fiction in an honest way knows that it is a process of discovery, like journalism in a foreign land. And I suspect that in Tolkien's literary hands, he had a feel for what could be put to use, even when it comes to a water fay. Perhaps then, it isn't so much that Goldberry has been domesticated as instead some latent good has been brought to the surface—like a recessive gene that is revealed in the red-headed child.

So, has Tom redeemed a water spirit? I can't say. All I can say is he's brought one home, and they seem happy enough. But I suspect that this is what Goldberry had always hoped for anyway. Perhaps that's the best description of redemption—the fulfillment of a longing, long suppressed. If that's so, then Tom truly is a master.

CHAPTER 6

"GET OUT, YOU OLD WIGHT! VANISH IN THE SUNLIGHT!"

IF TOM'S MASTERFUL handling of Old Man Willow and the Ring of Power left you wondering, *Just who is this guy?* what can we say about his encore with the Wight on the Barrow-downs?

Let's begin with some definitions. Just what is a down, what about a barrow, and what in the world is a Wight? The terms are all somewhat archaic.

Downland, according to Wikipedia, is an area "of open chalk hills... The term is used to describe the characteristic landscape in southern England... The name 'downs' is derrived from the Old English word dun, meaning 'hill.'"[1]

There's no mention of chalk-lands in *The Lord of the Rings* as far as I know, but the term *downland* can be used for any treeless, hilly, or rolling countryside. The Old Forest has its hills, ravines, and valleys, but those were forested. On the downs the hills continue, but without the trees.

So, what's a barrow? If you look it up you'll see a range of definitions. But the obvious meaning for this story is

---

1.Wikipedia, s.v., "downland," last modified November 15, 2020, https://en.wikipedia.org/wiki/Downland.

"a large mound of earth or stones over the remains of the dead."[2] So, it's a kind of tomb. And here on the Barrow-downs we have a graveyard of them, all on hills.

And finally, what's a Wight? This is the most interesting word of all. It originally meant *creature*, or a certain *person*, regarded as unfortunate. But it came to mean a "spirit" or a "ghost."

The Buildup

After leaving Tom's house, the hobbits must travel alongside this haunted graveyard in order to get back to the road that they must take if they are going to continue on their quest. Just who is entombed in the barrows, and what is haunting those tombs, becomes clear as the chapter is told. Tom knows the answers to both questions. After all, he saw the tombs raised.

But before the hobbits leave his house, Tom gives them this warning: "Don't you go a-meddling with old stone or cold Wights or prying in their houses, unless you be strong folk with hearts that never falter!"[3] He warns them more than once; and he advises them to pass the barrows by on their westward side. Then he teaches them a rhyme to sing just in case by ill-luck they fall into any danger.

Ho! Tom Bombadil, Tom Bombadillo!
By water, wood and hill, by reed and willow,
By fire, sun and moon, harken now and hear us!
Come, Tom Bombadil, for our need is near us![4]

2. Merriam-Webster, s.v. "barrow," accessed March 5, 2021, https://www.merriam-webster.com/dictionary/barrow.
3. *The Fellowship of the Ring*, 131.
4. *The Fellowship of the Ring*, 131.

Naturally the hobbits don't follow his advice. It says something about Tom's estimation of them that he felt the need to teach them the rhyme.

As the story goes, after saying goodbye to Tom and Goldberry, the hobbits set out with their five ponies. It's a warm day, and they're in good spirits, and after a morning of steady travel, they believe that they've made good progress. At noon, as hobbits are wont to do, they stop for lunch. But they make a terrible choice when it comes to where to have their picnic.

There are signs that things are not quite right with the place. We're told that the Forest seems to be smoking in the distance to their left, a mist rising from the hard rain of the previous day. And they come to a hill "whose top was wide and flattened, like a shallow saucer." From the top of this hill they look north and espy a dark line in the distance that they mistake for the road they are aiming for. The narrator remarks, "The distances had now all become hazy and deceptive." Then Frodo glances eastward and sees hills "crowned with green mounds, and on some were standing stones, pointing upwards like jagged teeth out of green gums."[5]

It turns out that those are not the only stones—there's one right in the center of the saucer they're in, "standing tall under the sun above.... It was shapeless and yet significant: like a landmark, or a guarding finger, or more like a warning."[6] But the hobbits don't heed the warning, and they forget Tom's warning as well about staying clear of old stone. They even lunch next to it, backs leaning up to it. They eat well, and then, unfortunately, they fall asleep. Tolkien hints that more may have been at work than eating too much and being too comfortable.

5. *The Fellowship of the Ring*, 133, 134.
6. *The Fellowship of the Ring*, 134.

What happens next seems to indicate that some wickedness was at work. They awaken very late in the afternoon, and the mist rising from the Forest, which was safely in the distance during their morning ride, has filled the entire area with dense fog. They quickly gather their things and lead their ponies down the north side of the hill. The air is like soup, and soon they are dripping wet and can't see where they are heading. Before long they're separated, and instead of passing through the valley they had seen proceeding in the direction of the road, Frodo finds himself passing between two huge standing stones he had not seen until that very moment. His pony rears and he falls off. Desperate, he wildly calls for his friends. He can hear them calling back from a distance, but ominously their voices are extinguished one by one with "a long wail suddenly cut short."[7]

Night falls and Frodo wanders aimlessly. Then the fog is at last blown away and Frodo finds himself on a round hilltop in front of a great barrow. He thinks that he hears a muted cry and he makes for it. He calls, "Where are you?" The answer, "here" seems to rise from the ground. Then a black silhouette against the star-illumined nighttime sky rises and looms over him. It has eyes, lit with a cool light, as from "some remote distance." Then the Wight—for that is what it is—takes a hold of him, and Frodo loses consciousness.[8]

When Frodo awakens he discovers that he is inside a barrow and that he is lying alongside Sam, Merry, and Pippin. The other hobbits are unconscious. What's more, by a "pale greenish light" glowing all around, he sees that they are clothed in white and bedecked with circlets of gold, and gold chains, and many rings. But most discon-

7. *The Fellowship of the Ring*, 136.
8. *The Fellowship of the Ring*, 136–37.

certingly, there is a naked sword lying across their necks. Then Frodo hears a chanting rhyme as from a great distance, rising from the ground:

Cold be hand and heart and bone,
and cold be sleep under stone:
never more to wake on stony bed,
never, till the Sun fails and the Moon is dead.
In the black wind the stars shall die,
and still on gold here let them lie,
till the dark lord lifts his hand
over dead sea and withered land.[9]

The Nature of Evil

The incantation mentions the Dark Lord. But we learn that the tombs were raised for the kings of the lost kingdom of Arnor. A little research reveals that the men laid in them were Númenóreans. The origin of the Wight isn't entirely clear, but there are hints that it is the spirit of one of the enemies of the kings of Arnor. Probably one of the men of Carn Dûm. That was a wicked place, located at the extreme northern reach of the Misty Mountains and subject to the Witch-realm of Angmar. The Witch-king who ruled there is one of the black Númenóreans, and a servant of Sauron. And he is none other than the chief of the Nazgul, the black riders in *The Lord of the Rings*, who are pursuing Frodo and his friends.

There is a great deal to think about here regarding the nature of evil. Calling it "the nature of evil" is ironic, because we think of nature as a place for living things—things with potential for growth and good, which by their natures contribute to the good of other things. But evil tends "naturally" towards death.

---

9. *The Fellowship of the Ring*, 138.

Look at the incantation for a moment; it is an exposition on the theme of death. Not only are hand, heart, and bone cold, the sun fails, and the moon and stars die. This is a picture of entropy, what scientists in our world bloodlessly call "heat death."

Just before we hear the incantation we are told that as the voice of the Wight grows intelligible, it seems, "immeasurably dreary"—and when the words grow distinct they are "grim, hard, cold words, heartless and miserable." If night could envy day, and cold, warmth, these are the words they would form to curse the things they are not.[10]

This is a good description of damnation, if the word *good* may be so employed. It is also painful to think about, in part because it describes you, or me, at our worst moments. There are things in us that really do deserve to go to Hell. The question is whether or not we will let those things take the rest of us with them.

The allusion to the Dark *Lord* is also worth pondering. What's the nature of the Wight's fealty? Is it devotion? Is it fear? Is it a common hatred for things with natures not subject to the Darkness? The mystery of ungodliness is great. The Dark Lord is a "lord"—he exercises a form of authority. And authority is good; it arises from the power of making. (*Author* and *authority* have six letters in common for a reason.)

Jesus said that even Satan keeps an ordered house (Matt. 12:22–28). But it must ape another rule of order, because evil by definition can't make anything good; it can only corrupt good things that have been made by someone else.

---

10. *The Fellowship of the Ring*, 137.

Hierarchy, Pandemonium, and the Bureaucracy of Hell

Hierarchy is another one of those words that has gotten nothing but bad press. It doesn't deserve it; it means "sacred-order"—and there's nothing sacred in Mordor. Yet in some sense Mordor is ordered, like the Devil's house. If we can ferret out how it is managed, perhaps we can redeem the word *hierarchy*, at least in our minds.

Just one more word to define before getting on with it: the word *pandemonium*. It literally means "devils everywhere." What we're referring to when we use it in everyday speech is chaos. Throughout *The Lord of the Rings*, when we get glimpses of the inner-workings of the forces of darkness, things do seem to be on the verge of breaking down into mere anarchy. So how does the Dark Lord hold it all together?[11]

Bureaucracy: namely, instrumental control and management.

C.S. Lewis reflected extensively upon the psychology of evil throughout his works, but one book stands out: *The Screwtape Letters*. In *The Screwtape Letters* a senior demon named Screwtape mentors a junior demon named Wormwood. The names are worth noting: Wormwood is a name you can find in the Bible; it connotes bitterness—the Hebrew literally means "curse." Screwtape, on the other hand is a bureaucrat, and I can't help thinking of "red-tape" when I hear his name. That wasn't a coincidence. Lewis found the impersonality and amorality of bureaucracy repellent. Here's a sample taken from the preface to *The Screwtape Letters*:

---

11. In *Morgoth's Ring*, the tenth volume of *The History of Middle-earth*, Tolkien had this to say about Sauron in the beginning: "He loved order and coordination, and disliked all confusion and wasteful friction...his 'plans', the idea coming from his own isolated mind, became the sole object of his will, and an end, the End, in itself" (396–97).

I live in a Managerial Age, in a world of "Admin." The
greatest evil is not done in those sordid 'dens of crime' that
Dickens loved to paint. It is not done even in concentration
camps and labour camps. In those we see its final result.
But it is conceived and ordered (moved, seconded, and
minuted) in clean, carpeted, warmed, and well-lighted
offices, by quiet men with white collars and cut finger
nails and smooth-shaven cheeks who do not need to raise
their voice. Hence, naturally enough, my symbol for Hell
is something like the bureaucracy of a police state or the
offices of a thoroughly nasty business concern.[12]

Tolkien evidently agreed with Lewis if we take his
description of the Shire near the end of *The Lord of the
Rings* as an indication of his thinking on the matter. The
Shire has been reduced to an over-managed industri-
al wasteland. Lists of rules are posted everywhere, and
thuggish and officious sheriffs confiscate the goods of
industrious hobbits and redistribute them—primarily to
themselves. Everything is controlled from Bag End (the old
home of Frodo and Bilbo), where Saruman, aka Sharkey,
now resides.

What keeps the hobbits in line is the same thing that
kept Wormwood in line. Years ago a mentor of mine let me
in on the secret. The primary emotion in any bureaucracy,
and the real thumbscrew of managerial control, is fear.

And this is why Heaven is not a bureaucracy. Instead, it
is a harmonious communion of natures, ruled by love. Hell,
by contrast, is managed by fear. In *The Screwtape Letters*,
when it comes to the end of that story, after Wormwood
fails to damn his patient, Screwtape relishes the thought
of consuming his charge. The idea apparently being that in
Hell there a food chain in which the higher consumes the

---

12. Preface to the 1961 edition, in C.S. Lewis, *The Screwtape Letters,* annot. ed.,
ed. Paul McCusker (1961; New York: HarperCollins, 2013), xxxvii.

lower. This is a reversal of the heavenly food chain we see in Christianity in which the highest of all gives himself as food for all, which results in a trickle-down of goodness and an expanding circumference of life.

Back to the Barrow

When Frodo awakens in the barrow and sees that his companions are "deathly pale," he thinks that his adventure has come to a "terrible end." It appears as though he and his friends are as good as dead.

Everyone dies. In the Christian faith death is a curse. But mysteriously, in *The Lord of the Rings* we're told that death is a gift from Illúvatar to his younger children, implying that something better is in store for them. Elves can die, but it is not inevitable, and in their case, it is not understood in the same way. But when it comes to men, a shadow of doubt weighs heavily upon men about it.[13]

The best that men (and hobbits) can do is meet it stoically, with an air of resignation. Anyone familiar with Stoicism can smell something like it in Frodo's resolution to face it heroically in the following passage:

> There is a seed of courage hidden (often deeply, it is true) in the heart of the fattest and most timid hobbit, waiting for some final and desperate danger to make it grow. Frodo was neither very fat nor very timid; indeed, though he did not know it, Bilbo (and Gandalf) had thought him the best hobbit in the Shire.[14]

---

13. In Tolkien's legendarium this is somewhat ambiguous—some among the Elves refer to death as Illúvatar's "gift" to men, his younger children. But men disagree, believing instead that Melkor had robbed them of lives similar to those lived by the Eldar, Illúvatar's older children. See *Morgoth's Ring*.
14. *The Fellowship of the Ring*, 137.

Then we're told that the thought of death "hardened" Frodo. He finds himself "stiffening, as if for a final spring"; he no longer feels limp, "like a helpless prey."[15]

But what can he do? When he sees a hand walking spider-like to the hilt of the sword lying across the necks of his friends, Frodo is tempted to flee. But his newly discovered courage won't allow it, so he takes another sword lying nearby and hacks the hand off. At this point the pale light goes out and he hears a "snarling noise."[16]

In spite of his courage, he has not saved himself or his friends at all. If possible, he's made things worse. So, he falls forward over Merry—and what he feels at that moment isn't courage; what he feels is Merry's deathly-cold face.

Then Frodo finally remembers Tom's silly song, and its promise:

Ho! Tom Bombadil, Tom Bombadillo!
By water, wood and hill, by the reed and willow,
By fire, sun and moon, harken now and hear us!
Come, Tom Bombadil, for our need is near us!

And he sings it. This is followed by a "sudden deep silence," as though the Wight, and even the world itself, are called to witness—along with the water and fire and everything else—something about to happen.

Then there is a response! Frodo hears faint, coming from a distance, as though passing through earth and stone the sound of someone else singing:

Old Tom Bombadil is a merry fellow,
Bright blue his jacket is, and his boots are yellow.

---

15. *The Fellowship of the Ring,* 137.
16. *The Fellowship of the Ring,* 138.

None has ever caught him yet, for Tom, he is the master;
His songs are stronger songs, and his feet are faster.[17]

Just how Tom could possibly have heard Frodo, we're
not told. Had he been looking for the hobbits? Did he
already know where they were? If so, why did he wait for
the song? We are not told that either. What we are told is
just how strong Old Tom's songs are.

> There was a loud rumbling sound, as of stones rolling
> and falling, and suddenly light streamed in, real light,
> the plain light of day. A low door-like opening appeared
> at the end of the chamber beyond Frodo's feet; and there
> was Tom's head (hat, feather, and all) framed against the
> light of the sun rising red behind him.[18]

Does this bring anything to mind? I can't help thinking
of Easter morning. And this brings us back to the question:
Who is this guy? Who is Tom Bombadil?

The End of the World

Many people have noted that the offices of Christ—prophet,
priest, and king—seem to correspond to particular characters in *The Lord of the Rings*: namely, Gandalf is like a
prophet, Frodo is like a priest, and obviously, Aragorn
really is a king.

However, the "return of the king" and the end of the
Ring of Power don't bring an end to evil in Middle Earth.
Instead, the end of *The Lord of the Rings* ushers in the Age
of Men, and the further greying of the world. The beauty
and heroism of the first three ages are reduced to legend
as the last of those for whom those were living memories

---

17. *The Fellowship of the Ring*, 138, 139.
18. *The Fellowship of the Ring*, 139.

leave Middle Earth. If this is all we had to go by in *The Lord of the Rings*, it would be a melancholy story, a last taste of good things never to be tasted again. But this isn't the only thing that we have to go by: there is Bombadil, and in particular, this scene, where he delivers the hobbits from the Shadow of Death.

When Tom appears he not only delivers the hobbits from the tomb; he does a number of other remarkable things, the most significant being this: he casts the Wight out of the tomb, and even beyond the circle of the world:

> *Get out, you old Wight! Vanish in the sunlight!*
> *Shrivel like the cold mist, like the winds go wailing,*
> *Out into the barren lands far beyond the mountains!*
> *Come never here again! Leave your barrow empty!*
> *Lost and forgotten be, darker than the darkness,*
> *Where gates stand for ever shut, till the world is mended.*[19]

Following this we're told there was, "a long trailing shriek, fading away into an unguessable distance; and after that silence."[20]

Well, if that isn't a picture of eternal damnation, I don't know what is. But there's more here to consider than that. We're given a hint of something glorious, "till the world is mended."

This line says something that's easy to overlook in our impatience to move on to the next stage of Frodo's adventure. It is a promise. There is a better ending to come—an ending that's better than the ending of *The Lord of the Rings*. Some day the world will be *mended*.

That world is not consigned to fiery obliteration, or even a slow, entropic process ending in a cold, eternal night. Instead, the darkness itself will be cast out. This

---

19. *The Fellowship of the Ring*, 139.
20. *The Fellowship of the Ring*, 139.

reminds me of the end of our world, as it is promised in the Bible. It is the damned who will "escape" to another world, when someone very like Tom here will cast them into the Outer Darkness. I would feel as though I'm reading too much into this episode if this were the only thing we had to go by in the body of Tolkien's work. But it isn't. There is something else, something I've referred to before in passing—something I believe that Tolkien wrote in order to console himself in the face of death. I'm thinking about his marvelous story *Leaf by Niggle*.

Leaf by Niggle

This story appears to have nothing to do with *The Lord of the Rings*. But I think it actually expresses Tolkien's hope for Middle Earth and much more.

Obviously, Tolkien was a maker of stories. People who make things can't help but wonder what will become of what they've made after they are gone. We all know about entropy; we see it everyday. Things fall apart; we fall apart. Even the best of us will die and eventually be forgotten. But what about our works, the books we've written, the paintings we've painted? Is it inevitable that everything will just fade away?

Ironically, as much as Tolkien looked down on allegory, many people believe that *Leaf by Niggle* is one. And it seems impossible to deny. The Niggle of *Leaf by Niggle* is a painter. And one painting has become an all-consuming project, a life's work—a painting of a vast tree. The painting keeps growing, and everything else he's painted is either forgotten or pinned to its edges. But the painting's scale, along with the distractions that lay claim to his time, cause Niggle to despair of ever finishing it.

Tolkien actually wrote *Leaf by Niggle* before *The Lord of the Rings* was published. And we know that even *The Lord of the Rings* was something tacked on to the edge of his great work—his legendarium. (Perhaps that is how Bombadil got into *The Lord of the Rings*.) Like Niggle, Tolkien felt that he was a niggler, and that he was niggling his life away. His vast legendarium might never be completed, or, perhaps worse, might be reduced to some practical purpose. (In *Leaf by Niggle* that's precisely what happens to Niggle's painting; the canvass it is painted on is used to patch a roof.)

In the story Niggle knows that he must eventually go on a journey that will put his labors to bed for good. (The journey is death; there's no doubt about it.) And wouldn't you know it, he does have to go before his painting is finished. And just as he feared, nearly everything he's worked on, so long and hard, is lost—everything, that is, except for one little leaf. The leaf manages to get a frame and find its way into a forgotten corner of a museum. (I can't help but think that Niggle's leaf was Tolkien's book, *The Hobbit*, because it was the only part of Tolkien's vast project that had actually been published by that time.)

But in *Leaf by Niggle* death isn't really the end—it's not even the end of Niggle's tree. Somehow the tree is there at the end of Niggle's journey, but it's no longer just a painting; instead, it's Real, and it's complete, and it's more wonderful than he ever envisioned.

The story can raise questions in the reader's mind (at least in my mind, anyway): is the tree there because Niggle painted it? Or was the tree there all along, and Niggle just saw it somehow and painted what he saw? We're not told. Perhaps the question is irrelevant in the great scheme of things.

It's a marvelous story, a consolation for makers, and rather than praising the next world at the expense of this one, *Leaf by Niggle* produces the opposite effect. It is because the world to come is more Real and Enduring than our world that our labors in this world matter. The next world infuses this one with meaning because, as the story suggests, in some sense our works in this world will follow us into the world to come.

Now, leaping back to jolly Tom—I suspect that something like this is the secret source of his infectious joy.

Tom's seen it all; nevertheless he sings and dances over water-lilies as though he's seeing them for the first time. Yes, he is able to feel melancholy, as, for example, when after delivering the hobbits from the Wight, he comes out of the tomb with an armful of treasure, and something in it brings someone to mind.

> He chose for himself...a brooch set with blue stones, many-shaded like flax-flowers or the wings of blue butter-flies. He looked long at it, as if stirred by some memory, shaking his head, and saying at last:
> 'Here is a pretty toy for Tom and for his lady! Fair was she who long ago wore this on her shoulder. Goldberry shall wear it now, and we will not forget her!'[21]

And just like that, jolly Tom is back.

Elves grow old, but they'll never be as old as Tom. And their melancholy doesn't fade with time; it only seems to grow. In a sense, their best days are behind them. They've fought a long defeat. But somehow Tom manages to live in the present. Could it be that it is because Tom knows how things end? Is that what gives his life between the Perilous Land and the Shadow of Death its lightness and joy?

---

21. *The Fellowship of the Ring,* 142.

You could say that we're more like hobbits lost in the Old Forest than we are like Tom Bombadil. As we travel along we see beautiful things, but also dark things—things full of malice for those "that go on two legs."[22] We're bewildered, over-matched, constantly opposed by obstacles, and our going is easy in only one direction: down, down, down to the last river; and we must cross it. And in the end we are surrounded by fog, the light goes out, and we're done.

But is that it? Is that the end?

Not if Someone very like Tom has something to say about it. There will be a day—a great getting-up morning—and a loud rumbling sound, as of stones rolling, and falling, and suddenly light will stream in, the Real Light of Day, and a Final Day will begin that will never end. And we will run free upon the grass of a world that will never fade.

---

22. *The Fellowship of the Ring*, 282.

CHAPTER 7

"I AM GOING TO HAVE A LONG TALK WITH BOMBADIL"

ALL GOOD THINGS must come to an end—that's the saying. And it applies to *The Lord of the Rings* as much as it does to anything else. I think that the success of Tolkien's posthumously published works—many of them unfinished, and stapled together by Tolkien's faithful son, Christopher—has a lot to do with the sweet and melancholy aftertaste that people want to linger once the story is over.

Having come to the end, can we accept it? Gandalf does. As we come near to the end of the story, and the hobbits are nearly home after many adventures, Gandalf warns them that one more adventure awaits them in the Shire. When the hobbits say that they have nothing to worry about because he is with them, the wizard says,

> 'I am with you at present,' said Gandalf, 'but soon I shall not be. I am not coming to the Shire. You must settle its affairs yourselves; that is what you have been trained for. Do you not yet understand? My time is over: it is no longer my task to set things to rights, nor to help folk to do so. And as for you, my dear friends, you will need no help. You are grown up now. Grown indeed very high;

among the great you are, and I have no longer any fear at all for any of you.

'But if you would know, I am turning aside soon. I am going to have a long talk with Bombadil: such a talk as I have not had in all my time. He is a moss-gatherer, and I have been a stone doomed to rolling. But my rolling days are ending, and now we shall have much to say to one another.'[1]

So Gandalf, the Grey Pilgrim, the rolling stone, finally comes to rest. That sounds sad, but Gandalf doesn't sound sad. He knows that something new and strange awaits him: rest.

The Problem of Rest

It is not uncommon for people to ask preachers, "Will we be bored in Heaven?" Leaving aside the unfathomable question of what Heaven is really like, and even whether or not the redeemed are actually destined to live there (or someplace new), I suspect that the real concern has to do with the meaning of life.

For most people the meaning of life is wrapped up with their work. But when the work is done, what then? For a saintly few, life's meaning is derived from the daily struggle with evil. (The feisty among us enjoy a good tussle.) But the Bible tells us that even that will come to an end someday. The good guys are going to win, finally, and forever. The fight will be over. Our Rest will be won.

So, what then? Will we just sit around reminiscing about our glory days like a bunch of former high school athletes? (We see something like this with Pippin and Merry according to an appendix in *The Lord of the Rings*.)

---

1. *The Return of the King*, 974.

There's another way of approaching the problem that sounds good, and even pious, but there's still something not quite right about it. I recall my wife's grandfather, a theologian with advanced degrees from Harvard and Yale, saying that Heaven would be like a library where study never ends. While I think that may be a little closer to the truth, I still think it misses by a long shot. When we see Cherubim in the Bible, it doesn't look like they're studying God in the way that theologians study Him. They're praising Him, and that's quite different. (More about this in a moment.[2])

But for the moment, let's return to the question, "Will Heaven be boring?" Perhaps it seems like it could be if you don't have a taste for holiness. (But if that's the case, Heaven would most likely be terrifying rather than boring.) The very question begs the question; it is also blasphemous because it implies that the creation has something that the Creator does not.

How can we imagine an eternal rest when we can't even rest for a few moments now? We may look forward to a vacation so that we can "rest and recuperate," but that way of putting it shows that the point of rest is getting back to work. Perhaps you've felt listlessness on the third week of vacation. That's when "sleeping in" has lost its charm, and you're looking for things to do. If Heaven is like that, it probably sounds like Hell. Perhaps eternal rest is unimaginable because it calls for an entirely different mode of life. I think that's what we see with Gandalf here—he needs to have a long talk with Bombadil because he's entering a mode of life for which Tom is truly the master.

---

2. The best theologians don't separate study from worship—I'm not talking about those theologians.

The Active and Contemplative Modes of Life

Medieval thinkers noted that life can be lived in two modes—an active life and a contemplative one. Ideally, a man ought to make time for both. But people being people means that one or the other tends to come more naturally to most of us. Because of the plain need to make a living, the active life is easy to justify. It's also more interesting to observe. Watching someone at prayer is about as interesting as watching paint dry. And books about contemplatives usually don't appeal to anyone but contemplatives, unless, that is, they record visions full of dragons and brimstone.

This has been called the Martha-Mary Problem. You may recall the story. Jesus had some friends named Lazarus, Martha, and Mary, and they were siblings. Lazarus doesn't come into this story, but hopefully you remember the drama of his raising ("Lazarus, come forth!"). This story is about his sisters. Today we might call Martha a type A personality. She was a doer, a planner, a woman who got things done. And like many people of this type, if you didn't look busy, she'd help you get busy. To her credit, things do need to get done.

In this story Jesus and a bunch of hungry disciples had just dropped in for dinner—so, someone had to feed them. But if it hadn't been that, there would have been something else, because there is always something that needs doing for the Marthas of the world. That's why this story is so important and why it has annoyed the Marthas of the world ever since. Because here, in the middle of all the preparations, Martha's sister, Mary, was just sitting around doing nothing—at least that's the way it appeared to Martha. Mary, you see, was leisurely listening to Jesus. Presumably Jesus was teaching. When Martha noticed

Mary just sitting there—doing nothing—she complained to Jesus, assuming, I think, that He would do the sensible thing and back her up. Instead, He surprised her by saying this: "Mary has chosen the good portion, which will not be taken away from her" (Luke 10:42). (I've often wondered what the hungry disciples thought of that.)

Gandalf, Aragorn, Frodo, and the Dragon

The Lord of the Rings isn't the story of Tom Bombadil. It's a story about a quest to rid the world of power untethered from goodness. The Ring of Power is raw power, power supposedly beyond good and evil, as Nietzsche put it. But power untethered from the restraining and directing influence of goodness is necessarily evil. There's no "beyond" when it comes to good and evil. It's one or the other; either power serves goodness, or it serves evil.

While Tom Bombadil is good, he's no Martha. In *The Lord of the Rings* there's no Bombadil option. Evil must be defeated; if it isn't, then even Tom will fall in the end, (the last, as he was the first).[3] It's a situation much like the one we face today. We may feel like Frodo, wondering why we can't just sit things out. But Frodo was no Bombadil, and neither are we. We also live in a world dominated by a Dark Lord, the Dragon in the book of Revelation. And even though Christians, including Tolkien, know that only the return of the King will put an end to the Dragon, there are roles for the rest of us to play in the story of his defeat.

But even those stories will come to an end. And hopefully, when our stories are told someday, they will end the way Bilbo thought a good story should end: "And he lived happily ever after to the end of his days."[4]

---

3. *The Fellowship of the Ring*, 259.
4. *The Fellowship of the Ring*, 32.

When the fight is over and the doing is done, our lives will necessarily look more like Mary's—or Bombadil's—than Martha's, or Gandalf's. Since that's the case, perhaps we should get a little practice in resting before then. If we do we will find that Heaven isn't boring after all. It's something we can look forward to. It may even look like life at Tom's house.

Now, as I come to the end of this book, it is time for the big reveal; it is time for me to tell you what I think Tom is for, as plainly and as directly as I can.

I think Tom is the ending, as in a happy ending.

What does this have to do with dominion? Well, bless my beard, it's the same thing! In the Bible God doesn't lay down His dominion when He rests on the seventh day; He enjoys what He has made. And Tom's dominion and his rest amount to the same thing.

Perhaps this seems unlikely, since we meet Tom at the beginning of the story, before things really get going. But I think that's the genius of Tom, and Tolkien. He comes at the beginning because he gives us a glimpse of the ending—the happy ending.

"Where Shall I Find Rest?"[5]

Throughout *The Lord of the Rings*, Frodo, Sam, and the other members of the fellowship find rest along the way. At first it's just the four hobbits; then a mysterious Ranger called Strider joins them. Then four more join in: Boromir, the man from the South; Gimli, a dwarf; Legolas, an Elf; and, of course, Gandalf. At first they all find rest at Rivendell. Then, after disaster in the Mines of Moria in which the Fellowship seems to have lost Gandalf for good, the

---

5. This is Frodo's question to Gandalf as they approach the Shire near the end of *The Lord of the Rings*. Even though he's nearing home, Frodo suspects that he will not find the Rest he longs for there.

remainder of the Fellowship find rest in Lothlórien. And after that the Fellowship is soon broken. There are brief respites along the way for the remnant of the Fellowship, but no genuine rest, just smaller and smaller samples of the real thing until they all get to the end of the story. And even at the end of the story, Frodo doesn't find rest, not truly. He's too deeply wounded by his contest with evil. His hurts revisit him annually. He's restless, even in Bag-End. Only Sam truly understands. But Sam is torn; he's still very much at home in Middle-Earth. What's Frodo to do?

A truly great storyteller knows how to suggest the ending at the very beginning without giving too much away. We see that in the Bible, in something known as the proto-evangelium (Gen. 3:15). (In a way that's an entirely different story—but in another way it isn't.) And we have the ending of *The Lord of the Rings*, and the end of Frodo's story, faintly suggested in the house of Tom Bombadil. In the first paragraph in the chapter titled, "Fog on the Barrow-downs," we read this:

> That night they heard no noises. But either in his dreams or out of them, he could not tell which, Frodo heard a sweet singing running in his mind: a song that seemed to come like a pale light behind a grey rain-curtain, and growing stronger to turn the veil all to glass and silver, until at last it was rolled back, and a far green country opened before him under a swift sunrise.[6]

I suppose you could write this off as filler, or just a way of setting a scene to contrast with the action when the hobbits are captured by the Barrow-wight, if not for one thing. Frodo sees the vision in his dream again, this time at the very end of *The Lord of the Rings*. But this time he's

---

6. *The Fellowship of the Ring*, 132.

not dreaming—he's sailing into the West, and it is at this point that Bombadil is mentioned for the last time.

> And the ship went out into the High Sea and passed into the West, until at last on a night of rain Frodo smelled a sweet fragrance on the air and heard the sound of singing that came over the water. And then it seemed to him that as in his dream in the house of Bombadil, the grey rain-curtain turned all to silver glass and was rolled back, and he beheld white shores and beyond them a far green country under a swift sunrise.[7]

When Bilbo tells Frodo and Sam in Rivendell that books should have good endings, Sam raises a question: Where will the people who live 'happily ever after' live?[8] Well, now we know, they will live in a "far green country under a swift sunrise."

I could say more, but why should I? This is the end—Frodo's Eternal Rest—and nothing more that I could say could be better than that.

The End

---

7. *The Return of the King*, 1007.
8. *The Fellowship of the Ring*, 267.

POSTSCRIPT

"But why didn't Bombadil just take the Ring to Mordor himself and save Frodo all the trouble?"

When people learned that I was writing a book on Tom Bombadil, I heard some version of that question from the more knowledgeable of Tolkien's devotees. It's a fair question, and one that was even asked at the Council of Elrond: "'Could we not...obtain his help?' asked Erestor. 'It seems that he has a power even over the Ring.'"[1]

It's a comic image, even an endearing one: Technicolor Tom fearlessly skipping up the mountain path into the Dark Land, singing his nonsense songs, sending Shelob scurrying, and Orcs—or worse—running away with their hands over their ears, until finally, after stomping up the side of Mount Doom in his yellow boots, he casually flings the Ring of Power into its fiery cracks, after which he stands back, to watch the Dark Tower, and everything else made with the power of the Ring, just melt away.

Could he have done it? Gandalf didn't think so—but not because he lacked the power to do it, but because he'd forget to.

---

1. *The Fellowship of the Ring*, 259.

Gandalf's answer has never satisfied me.

Still, I'm glad Tom didn't do it; and I'm glad that he wasn't asked to. That story wouldn't have been nearly as good as the one we have. Perhaps that's the point—it wouldn't have been a good story. And maybe the same point applies to our world, and even to our lives. Our troubles, our daily struggles with evil, amount to a better story than one in which our troubles vanish with a casual wave of the Divine Hand.

Frodo wondered why he was given such a difficult task; remember: "I am not made for perilous quests. I wish I had never seen the Ring! Why did it come to me? Why was I chosen?"[2]

Gandalf tells Frodo that it is impossible to answer a question like that. People don't have everything that they need before beginning a perilous quest. They must learn on the job. They begin with what they have and rise to the challenges they face along the way.

Frodo didn't want to be a hero. He didn't long for glory; he wasn't Achilles, or even Boromir. But by the end he had risen very high—he was among the great of Middle Earth. Maybe not wanting to be great is a prerequisite of greatness. That's an encouraging thought, at least for those who read about the trials of others while comfortably seated by a fire, with a beer at the elbow, and a pipe in the mouth.

Callings

Each one of us has something sitting right in front of us that really must be done, but we'd rather not do. Other people are meant for other things. But that hasn't stopped

---

2. Frodo is mistaken, we come to see. He was made for a perilous quest. But it takes the rest of the story to make him the man (or the hobbit) for the job. That's the way being made for perilous quests works—it's on-the-job training.

anyone from saying, "I'd rather do what he's supposed to do. Why can't I do that?"

Callings come with boundaries, and Bombadil appears to be content with his. As Gandalf said, he lived within the boundaries of a little land.

But even Frodo had a Tookish side, a longing for adventure—for going places, and seeing things, for being swept up in something that would carry him far away. And it really was a nasty, uncomfortable adventure that made him great.

But travel isn't the only adventure. Sometimes staying put is all the adventure anyone could ask for; doing the thing that must be done, that only you can do—that's the real adventure. G. K. Chesterton amusingly begins his classic, *Orthodoxy*, with an account of an "English yachtsman who slightly miscalculated his course and discovered England under the impression that it was a new island in the South Seas."[3] Chesterton's point is that we already are somewhere strange and fascinating enough to satisfy anyone romantic enough to long for adventure. But do we see it?

Seemingly, Bombadil did. And it wasn't as though the coming of the Dark Lord was the first time that he'd seen the world go to Hell. He'd seen worse. When he spoke of the Dark Lord from the Outside, he wasn't thinking of Sauron. He was speaking of someone even darker, and more powerful. Presumably he had something else to do in those days, too, beside save the world. And in *The Lord of the Rings* he is content to let Frodo save Middle Earth. But that didn't prevent him from saving Frodo—twice. (So, it could be said that Tom actually saved Middle Earth—

---

3. *Orthodoxy*, Christian Heritage Series (1908; Canon Press, 2020), 4.

twice.[4]) But he did that by staying home and doing what needed doing when only he could do it.

And that is an encouraging thought.

---

4. Here's a postscript to the postscript, a final thought that occurred to me as I was putting the last touches on this book: the first time that Tom saved the hobbits it was at a tree, and the second time that he saved them it was at a tomb. For those pondering what Tom represents, that's an even more encouraging thought.